revised edition

Interviewing in Social Work Practice: An Introduction

Margaret Schubert
University of California, Berkeley

Council on Social Work Education
New York

Council on Social Work Education
Richard A. English, President
Arthur J. Katz, Executive Director
111 Eighth Avenue, New York, New York 10011
(212) 242-3800

Contents

Foreword

The Council on Social Work Education is pleased to publish this revised edition of Professor Margaret Schubert's important, durable contribution to social work literature. The tool of interviewing was one of the earliest developed and is the best of the social work profession's and one which continues to play a significant role in all aspects of this profession's practice.

Skill in interviewing is a key to a direct response to one of social work's basic principles — individualization. The knowledge base, which supports the development of skill in interviewing and with corresponding techniques, has been shared by social work in a number of other human service professions.

This revision, after eleven years, represents an attempt by the author to respond to changes in society and the institutions which are its agents. This revised edition, therefore, should be most useful in the education of contemporary social work.

New York City
ARTHUR J. KATZ
Executive Director
Council on Social Work Education

Preface
to the
Revised Edition

Scope of the Revision

This revision includes new material that has become increasingly important since the first edition was prepared eleven years ago, and eliminates some anachronisms. The sections on recording, confidentiality, and the various obstacles to mutual understanding between client and worker have been expanded and reorganized, and a brief new section on the use of telephone calls and letters has been added. The basic purpose of the book remains unchanged: to offer practical help to beginning interviewers in their efforts to gain competence in working with individuals and families.

Relevance of Principles of Interviewing

The one-to-one interview is a central means of working with individuals, and is frequently used in connection with helping family groups and formed groups. Interviews with persons in the environment on behalf of individual clients also form part of this helping method. Processes called "casework" and "groupwork" cannot be as neatly separated as they once were, and they are now often subsumed under such terms as "counseling," "micro-services," or "direct services." It is obvious that principles of interviewing should be understood in working with individuals, families, and formed groups, although family treatment and group counseling also require additional skills.

It is less obvious that interviewing forms a part of the professional social worker's activity in other aspects of practice. Administrators at various levels, community organizers, social planners, researchers, and consultants are not primarily concerned with giving direct help to a particular client, but rather are concerned with problems of policy, its administration, and evaluation of its results. They are involved in working with community groups and in helping other professionals give maximum services to the client. Specialists in these forms of practice are offering "indirect services" — they are rarely in personal contact with the individual recipient of service. Nevertheless, they are constantly engaged in talking with individuals and groups in an effort to achieve a mutual understanding of a task to be accomplished or an issue to be resolved. Administrators who fail to pay attention to what staff members are saying or fail to understand the point of view of board members will be unable to carry out their functions successfully.

There are few professional positions that permit one to work in isolation for any extended period of time. Researchers are sometimes thought of as solitary types whose principal relationships are with computers, but some of the most difficult tasks involved in research involve making arrangements with others in order to achieve a mutual understanding of the purpose of a project, the kinds of data to be gathered, and the method of gathering such data. Then, if interviews are to be the method of data-gathering, special skills are needed. When caseworkers (accustomed to using the interview as a helping method) are employed as research interviewers, it is all too easy for them to engage in a helping process, and sometimes they fail to recognize the extent to which their conduct of the interview can affect the nature of the data they collect and can affect the persons whom they interview.

In supervision and case consultation, the lines between administration, teaching, and counseling functions can become blurred. This is most likely to happen when problems in the worker's own self-awareness are the subject of the conference. Because a degree of self-understanding is essential on the part of interviewers, it may be necessary to discuss some aspect of this when the supervisor or consultant tries to help workers deal with their feelings in the interest of the client. Here it is more than ever important that the purpose of the conference be recognized by the persons concerned. If goals are ambiguous or if there is disagreement about the objectives, it is improbable that the process will be fruitful.

There are many publications that deal with the areas of practice mentioned above, and no attempt will be made here to cover this large and complex subject matter. I suggest, however, that many of the concepts presented are applicable in aspects of social work other than that of direct service to individual clients.

Note on Terminology

The terminology of social work changes constantly: new terms come into favor, and old terms fall into disrepute. I continue to use the word "worker" interchangeably with caseworker, social worker, interviewer, or practitioner, and I continue to use "client" to designate the person to whom services are offered. I have avoided the substitutes "helper" and "helpee" that are currently found in some of the relevant literature.

The names given to the various practice methods still pose a problem. The "micro/macro" and "direct/indirect" classifications are less than precise, but are at least more satisfactory than such terms as casework, groupwork, and community organization, which (as noted in the Preface to the First Edition) sounded outmoded even eleven years ago.

References

Notes appear following each chapter. The Bibliography at the end of the book, arranged alphabetically by author, includes all the works cited, as well as a few books of general import not specifically noted in the text. My efforts to reduce the number of references have not met with resounding success.

Acknowledgements

I am indebted to many former colleagues with whom I consulted about needed revisions. Glenn Haworth of San Diego State University arranged a conference with a group of faculty members who were particularly helpful in contributing their knowledge of the problems of crossracial and crosscultural interviewing. Genevieve B. Oxley of the University of California, Berkeley, thoroughly reviewed the first edition, offered her ideas for revisions, and shared her bibliography. The faculty of the School of Social Work, Virginia Commonwealth University, sent me their relevant course outlines and extensive class bibliographies. Dorothy Pettes and Marie Ellert (who used the first edition in their class and field teaching at the University of Newcastle-upon-Tyne, England) read the first draft of the revised edition with meticulous care and offered useful suggestions for alterations. Hans Falck, chairperson of the Publications Committee of the Council on Social Work Education, also helped me cope with some of the problematic aspects of revision. To all these, and to the many others with whom I conferred more briefly, my thanks.

Preface
to the
First Edition

Scope of the Book

Social workers commonly use the interview as a major means of communication with persons they are trying to help. Like other aspects of real life, such encounters are to varying degrees chaotic, and the interviewer is faced with the task of making sense out of the interchange and reducing the chaos to proportions that the participants can encompass. Clearly there are the dangers of distorting meaning or imposing an artificial form that impedes mutual understanding. How can these dangers be minimized, and how can the interviewer contribute to a productive process? These are the questions to which this volume is addressed. The factors affecting the character of the interview will be enumerated, common types of interviews will be discussed, and the dimensions that must be taken into account will be presented. Further, there will be consideration of the ways in which major theories of helping affect the content and direction of the interview. The focus, however, will be on what the interviewer can put into the process under given conditions.

Our concern is with the interview as a means of helping the persons to whom social services are offered. Social workers, in their roles as administrators, supervisors, givers and receivers of consultation, collaborators, and participants in research, also use interviews in carrying out their tasks. Although such interviews have something in common with the "helping" interview, their purposes and forms differ substantially, and they will be discussed only briefly.

Note on Terminology

A number of terms commonly used in the social work literature are currently in disfavor, but no satisfactory substitutes have yet been found. To some practitioners (but not to the writer) the word "client" has a derogatory connotation, yet this seems to be the only word that can be substituted for the awkward circumlocution "person to whom social services are offered," and it will be used in this sense. "Agency" is another word that presents some difficulty, for today's social work practice is carried out in many settings that do not fit the conventional picture of a social agency. In this book, "agency" refers to the setting or the auspices of the social service and not merely to the traditional established social agency. Finally, for lack of a better term, the word "worker" (which unfortunately calls to mind the picture of an ant hill) will be used interchangeably with interviewer, practitioner, and social worker.

The terms used to designate various methods of practice present a problem of a different order. There was once a grain of truth in the stereotypes of casework (the fifty-minute hour), groupwork (games and crafts with adolescents), and community organization (staffing committees from the establishment), but concepts of social work practice are undergoing a marked change. The current scene is characterized by ambiguity and conflict of ideas about the meaning of casework, groupwork, and community organization so that the words themselves have an old-fashioned sound. As used in this volume, "casework" refers to the help offered individuals and families, when the interview is the primary method; "groupwork" refers to those helping methods in which the focus is on the group itself, with the individual interview as a supplemental means of helping group members in their use of the group; and "community organization" refers to work with neighborhood organizations as well as social planning groups, with individual interviews and group discussions as the means by which the worker helps people get something done in the community.

The point of view taken here is that although individual interviews are an essential part of all three modes of practice, there are some identifiable differences related to the context in which such interviews take place and the purpose to which they are directed. The "generalist" social worker, as well as those who see themselves as specialists in one method of practice, need to be aware of these differences.

Acknowledgements

This book is a combination of advice to interviewers and an attempt to explain why some things seem to work. It stems from my experience in thousands of interviews and my efforts to make sense out of the experience. I have learned many things from my clients in ways that cannot be documented precisely, but one example is illustrative: I recall with relish a situation in which I had assisted an unmarried mother during her pregnancy, delivery, and placement of the child, and I had a rather vague notion that interviews would continue. The client, however, had a clear picture of the nature of the contract, and wrote me a letter thanking me for my help, reviewing what had been accomplished, and announcing her own plans for the immediate future — a concise closing summary.

My indebtedness to teachers and colleagues is inadequately reflected in the Bibliography. Charlotte Towle, Helen Harris Perlman, and Lilian Ripple have been especially important influences through their writing, their classroom discussions, and numerous informal conferences.

I have consulted with many persons, formally or casually, during the preparation of this volume. I wish to acknowledge particularly the help given by the staff of Eastern State Hospital, Williamsburg, Virginia, where Charles Nimmo and Barbara Palmer discussed with me some of the needs of inexperienced interviewers and gave me an opportunity to talk at length with several beginning workers. Dean Richard Lodge and Emanuel Tropp of the School of Social Work, Virginia Commonwealth University, and Daniel Grodofsky of the Council on Social Work Education have assisted materially in suggesting concepts and illustrations from groupwork. Eleanor Ryder of CSWE was a major resource in relation to the use of the interview in community organization. Grodofsky and Ryder, along with other members of the CSWE staff, generously assisted me in selecting the focus and setting the limits of the presentation of interviewing. To all these, my thanks.

Chapter

1

Definition
of an Interview

The word "interview" evokes a picture of at least two people talking together with some purpose in mind. One of the older definitions of the term is peculiarly applicable to the social work interview: "a mutual sight or view."[1] These concepts of mutuality and purposeful talking are fundamental to an interview that is geared to helping people.

Who does the talking? How is the purpose determined? How is mutuality achieved? The rather unsatisfactory answer to these questions is that "it depends" — depends on a complex constellation of factors that focus on the nature of the problem or task at hand, the persons who feel some concern about it, the auspices under which help is being offered, the psychological, cultural, and social attributes of the persons involved in the interview, and the physical setting in which the interview takes place.[2]

One stereotyped image of a social work interview consists of something like this: a person comes to an agency office

1

after arranging an appointment with the receptionist, arrives at the specified time, is ushered into a caseworker's private office, explains clearly what the purpose of the visit is, spends an hour in discussing the problem or situation (volunteering information and responding to questions), and is given another appointment for the following week.

There are several things wrong with this picture:

1. The contact with the social worker is not always initiated by the client.
2. The client often is unable to state the problem or request clearly, or may not think a problem exists.
3. Worker and client may not understand each other.
4. The interview may include several persons.
5. The length of an interview can vary widely; a significant contact may last for five minutes or several hours.
6. A single interview may be the sole contact between client and worker, or there may be a series of interviews regularly or irregularly spaced over a period of weeks, months, or even years.
7. Interviews take place in many settings other than a conventional office: for example, in homes, hospital rooms, waiting rooms, automobiles, bus stations, airports, coffee shops, prisons, or the dayrooms of mental hospital wards.
8. Interviewing is an inescapable part of all social work practice and is not limited to casework in agencies whose primary purpose is helping individuals and families. It is an adjunct to working with small groups, to helping community groups, to administration and supervision, and to research.

Notes

1. Webster's *New International Dictionary,* 2nd ed., unabridged (Springfield, Mass.: G. & C. Merriam Co., 1957), p. 1301.

2. Two books on interviewing have become classics in the social work literature: Annette Garrett, *Interviewing: Its Principles and Methods,* 2nd ed. (New York: Family Service Association of America, 1972); and Alfred Kadushin, *The Social Work Interview* (New York: Columbia University Press, 1972). Garrett's book was originally published in 1942 and much of the original text is unchanged. Also see the chapter on "Suggestions for Practice" in Alan Keith-Lucas, *Giving and Taking Help* (Chapel Hill, N. C.: University of North Carolina Press, 1972). Numerous texts on casework, counselling, psychotherapy, and behavior modification also contain useful ideas on interviewing, and these are listed in the Bibliography.

Chapter 2

Getting Started: The Concept of a 'Contract'

Let us first consider what may happen in interviews initiated by clients. These are situations in which individuals (or perhaps two or more members of a family) have somehow reached the decision that they want to ask for help from a particular agency. Usually much has occurred between the time that the first twinge of discomfort is felt and the time that the contact with a social worker takes place, and all these events will affect the content and direction of the interview. Clients bring with them not only the problem as they define it, but also their experience in trying to solve it, their feelings about it, their prior attempts at solution, and their feelings about asking for help. Interviewers are at once faced with two major tasks: they must make it possible for clients to talk about their concerns, and they must make sure that they understand what the clients are telling them about the problem at hand.

Rules of Interviewing: How To Begin

There are a few rules that are helpful to interviewers in carrying out the two major tasks:

1. Give the client your full attention.
2. Don't jump to conclusions.
3. When you don't understand the client, ask for clarification.

The beginning social worker, anticipating a first interview, may say: These rules are all very good, but how shall I start this interview? What do I say? What if the client doesn't talk?

When the clients have initiated the first contact, the chances are that they have rehearsed in their own minds what they are going to say, that they will feel some urgency about saying it, and that they will start saying it as soon as the initial greeting is over. One might note here that the usual courtesies of greeting clients are sometimes so automatic that we are scarcely aware of their importance in establishing communication. To speak to people by name is to recognize them as individuals and is one symbol of giving them our full attention. To show clients to a chair, to make sure that the light is not glaring into their eyes, to take their coat — these are gestures that indicate ordinary human concern for the clients' comfort.

Clients may need no further encouragement to talk. If they make no attempt to begin, the worker might ask a neutral question, such as: "Can you tell me about it?" Or, "What is on your mind?" Or, "How can we help you?" The reason for trying to phrase the question in a neutral fashion is that at this point in a beginning contact the worker really does not know what the matter is, how serious the problem may be, or what the client's feelings about it are. The worker tries to avoid questions that will make clients feel that they have to present themselves in a particular way and consequently distort their true request. Such an initial misunderstanding may be a temporary or protracted obstacle to effective help.

Here are some examples of the opening statements of different clients:

Somebody should do something about my boy—he skips school and won't mind me and I know he will get in trouble.

I just can't go on any longer. I can't take it, my wife can't take it and the kids can't take it—I have got to get dad into a nursing home or something, and I can't possibly pay for it.

I'm confused about what I have to do to get unemployment insurance; people tell me different things.

I'm not sure I'm in the right place but I have three problems: marital, financial, and medical.

I've got to get Danny into a foster home; he is wrecking my nerves.

My relief check didn't come.

I've lost my ticket and I have got to get back to Omaha but I suppose nobody will help me.

I've got marital problems and I want counseling of some kind but I don't want to tell my story over and over. First I want to know what your qualifications are.

I'm worried about my husband. I don't know what to do. He is acting very strange.

Problems such as these are presented to a wide variety of social agencies: public assistance agencies, Travelers Aid, medical clinics, mental health clinics, family agencies, child placement agencies, and others. These clients have identified some sort of discomfort or uncertainty in vital areas of their lives. Their initial statement may be in terms of a problem, a proposed solution, or a combination of these; they may place the problem within themselves or attribute its origin to others; they may ask help so that they can deal with the problem or they may ask others to take over the responsibility. Some ask for relatively simple information, some ask for specific agency services, and some express confused bewilderment; some ask timidly or even subserviently and some present an angry challenge.

Agency Services Related to Clients' Requests

One of the things that clients need to know as quickly as possible is whether the agency they have selected is the most appropriate place to seek help with the problem as they have defined it. Clients may be very well-informed about the services offered by the agency either through their own prior experience or that of acquaintances, but the worker cannot take this for granted. The worker needs to listen to or elicit enough of a client's story to get a fairly clear understanding of whether the situation is one in which that particular agency has a relevant service to offer. If it becomes apparent that the agency cannot be of assistance, the worker will need to take active steps with the client in planning for an application elsewhere. Clients may justifiably feel cheated and deceived if they are encouraged to unburden themselves extensively only to be told at the end of the conversation that the agency is unable to help and that they will have to tell their story again somewhere else. In other words, in this initial phase of the first interview the worker needs to let the client talk enough but not too much; to ask enough questions but not too many. The purpose is to reach some tentative decision about the appropriateness of agency services.

It often is appropriate to ask questions, not only in the initial interview, but also in later interviews. Direct questions are useful when precise information is needed about such things as names, dates, and addresses. But in helping clients elaborate on the nature of their problem, their feelings about it, and their hopes and fears, interviewers should try to keep their questions openended. Questions that can be answered simply by "yes" or "no" lead nowhere. In general, questions that help clients talk about *what* happened, or *how* it happened, will open up the discussion; questions about *why* it happened usually are unanswerable; and questions that embody the worker's answer (either explicitly or implicitly) put an end to the topic. Some examples of productive and unproductive questions are:

> What was happening when the teacher got so mad at you?
>
> Why did you talk back to the teacher?
>
> You really didn't intend to make the teacher mad, did you?

The first question focuses on specific events and actions, and could lead the client to a better understanding of a troublesome situation. The second question imputes blame, and the client probably doesn't yet know the answer to this. The third question tells the client that the worker wants to hear the reply, "No, I didn't intend to make the teacher angry."[1]

In this initial exploration, interviewers should guard against the assumption that the particular service they are equipped to offer is in fact an appropriate service in response to the client's request. When the client asks for emergency financial assistance and the agency's only service is arranging for adoption of children, the incompatibility between the request and the service is immediately apparent. When, however, a mother comes to a family agency complaining that her ten-year-old son is having difficulty in school, it should by no means be taken for granted that extended individual counseling with the mother in this agency is an appropriate method of helping. Does the child have a physical or mental handicap? Is he in the right grade for his capacities? Are there factors in the school situation that can and should be altered? Does the child need the help of a group in learning to get along with peers? A full assessment of the problem situation might suggest a number of alternatives: consultation with school personnel, work with the whole family, individual work with the child, referral to another agency for medical or psychiatric care, for remedial teaching, or for group experiences.

Listening and Observing

The worker listens to what clients say and also observes the way in which they say it. Feelings may be expressed through body posture, voluntary body movement, involuntary responses (such as flushing, sweating, stuttering, coughing), as well as in the tone of voice and pace of speech. The interviewer pays attention to all of these things, trying to understand the situation and the clients' feelings about it. One should be particularly alert here to the connections between what the clients are saying and their other expressions of feeling. A simple request for information accompanied by a flood of tears suggests that the problematic situation in back of the request is troublesome and that the client may wish to discuss it more fully. In other instances, a client may in very subtle ways indicate powerful feelings about a subject but keep them under tight control in an effort to give a rational and coherent account of the problem. One also must remember that people react differently to situations that on the surface appear alike. An event that might have tremendous impact on the worker could be viewed much less seriously by a client, and an event that seems trivial to the worker might have deep import for a client. The purpose of trying to understand clients' feelings about what they are saying is to be able to respond appropriately without minimizing or exaggerating the problem.

Establishing a Working Relationship and a Tentative Contract

Let us assume that in the first ten or fifteen minutes of this initial interview it becomes clear to the worker that the client has come to the right agency and that some service can be offered. The client then needs to know what service can be given and who is going to give it. The client also needs to know what the conditions of this assistance are: whether certain eligibility requirements have to be met, how much time is going to be involved, whether a fee will be charged, or whether it will be necessary to be in contact with other persons connected with the problem situation. Does the worker see any hope of helping the client in meeting the request or some part of it? Who is supposed to do what in the immediate future, and what bearing will this have on the problem the client has presented? Clarity about these points is the basis for the client's decision about using the services of the agency. The understanding between the worker and the client is a kind of tentative contract—a contract that needs to be reconsidered as changes in the situation take place.[2]

This beginning interchange between client and worker is the starting point of a relationship—a connection with a purpose. During this period, as well as later, the interviewer offers reassurance. This is expressed through a willingness to listen, a realistic appraisal of the problem, a recognition of whatever strength the client has demonstrated, and a hope for a solution to the problem or an amelioration of a troublesome situation. To hold out false expectations or to tell the client that everything will be all right when this is manifestly improbable constitutes impediments to the development of confidence. If the client believes the worker, disillusionment will ensue; and if the client does not believe the worker, contacts probably will be discontinued.

Engaging the Client Who Seeks Help

Sometimes working out the contract is a simple matter. A man in his late sixties whose retirement benefits are grossly inadequate to meet basic living costs requests supplementary financial assistance. He presents no problem other than financial need. But he has to know the kind of evidence of age that is required and the kind of inquiry regarding financial and family resources that will be made. He needs to know about how long it will take to process the application and how much money he will receive if the application is acted on favorably. He needs to know what his responsibility is in taking next steps, and what steps will be initiated by the worker. A discussion of these matters may be quite straightforward. The client is in reasonably good health, he has a place to live, and he has resources that will last him until the application is acted on. He evinces no particular distress over the necessity of asking for financial assistance. In such instances the nature of the contract is clear to both parties and easily achieved.

Sometimes, however, a host of additional problems emerges even in this early phase of reaching an understanding with the client about the service that can be given and the conditions under which it will be given. For example, this client may have brought with him the family Bible in which his birth date is inscribed, and a copy of his savings account passbook that shows a balance of $20. He may have these documents with him with the expectation that his application will be accepted immediately and a check issued within a week. The prospect of delay may create panic or rage or a sense of helplessness. In such a situation it is not unusual for the client to accuse the worker or the agency of willfully withholding funds. It is never comfortable to be the recipient of such direct animosity, but it is easier to take if workers keep their minds on the meaning of the anger rather than on defending themselves.

The client's rage may represent a number of different things. It could be an expression of his own sense of defeat after having spent a long life working for marginal wages. It could represent a genuine fear of a realistically hazardous immediate future with uncertainty about housing and food for the next few weeks. Or it could even mean that the client is falsifying his application and is afraid of being found out.

What should the worker say or do in response to a verbal attack? A counterattack and the resulting sparring match are fruitless, nor does it do any good to pretend that the anger does not exist. Sometimes a simple acknowledgement of this state of feeling is sufficient: "I can see you are pretty mad about this." This may be enough to help the client start talking more productively about what the situation is and what can be done about it. At other times the worker may have a clearer idea of what is troubling the client most seriously and can say in so many words: "I know you are very worried about the rent payment which is due next week. Let's see exactly what the situation is and whether anything can be done to work this out." Occasionally it even may be useful for workers to admit their own discomfort: "It's kind of upsetting to know that you are so mad at me, but I can see you are really worried about something. Can you tell me what it is?"

Similarly, when clients lie it does no more good for workers to pounce on the lie with vindictive precision than to pretend to believe it. Some lies the client will voluntarily correct and some are so trivial they can be set aside, but there are times when workers have to confront the client with their knowledge of the facts. This is part of the effort to understand the meaning of the client's behavior and the purpose it serves.

What workers actually say and do in these situations depends both on their perception of the clients' feelings and their perception of their own feelings and ability to manage them in the interest of the clients. In the attempt to move the interview into productive channels, the objective is to engage clients as quickly as possible in the facts of their situation and in the things that they and the worker can do about it in a practical way.

Other problems may emerge in the course of this early discussion of the agency's services and the client's obligations. A requirement that other members of the household be interviewed may bring out problems in family relationships that clients need to talk about before they can continue with their application. The aged father who is dependent on his married children may express both positive and negative feelings. He may fear that his presence in the home is an excessive emotional burden or he may fear that the financial support his children are giving him is beyond their means. He may resent his dependence on them and fear that he cannot call his life his own unless he has an income from another source. On the other hand, he may express resentment toward his children for what he sees as rejection of him and refusal to give him the assistance that they could well afford.

For the interviewer this poses another kind of problem in deciding on appropriate activity. One thing to keep in mind is that feelings are rarely purely negative or positive. Clients who initially present an extremely negative picture of their relatives are likely at a later point to start talking about some of the positives. Similarly, the client who paints a glowing picture of the perfect daughter-in-law in the first interview may well reveal a number of uncertainties about her at a later time. What is important for interviewers to keep in mind is that they do not want to lock clients into their story, nor do they want to ignore the content of the initial discussion. The rule in general is to accept the story without reinforcing it in such a way that at a later point the client would find it difficult to tell other aspects of the story. Even the most experienced interviewer is caught up in the drama of the initial presentation and sometimes finds it hard to maintain sufficient neutrality to avoid what may become a distortion.

The example given here is a relatively simple one. That is, the client has initiated the contact with the agency and has defined a problem with which the agency can offer help. It seems reasonable to expect that the client and the worker can reach a mutual understanding of the nature of the problem, the services of the agency, and the conditions under which the services are to be offered. Even here it is apparent that clients who present similar requests are in fact highly individual and need different responses from the worker.

Engaging the 'Unwilling' Client

It is not always the client who initiates the contact or defines the problem. Persons may be forced into the presence of the social worker for a number of reasons: their family's concern, society's desire to protect itself against them, or society's desire to protect them from their own self-destructive behavior or from the destructive behavior of others. The teenage delinquent is likely to say: "I wasn't doing anything, I was just standing there." The father who abuses his child may say: "This is my son and he needs to learn to mind me, and this is none of your business." How can interviewers start with such persons? How can they engage them in a discussion that has any meaning or purpose? How can they arrive at a tentative contract when these people profess no need for help and actively resent their presence? The lack of conscious positive motivation is an impediment to the use of help; denial of a problem makes it difficult to arrive at a mutual view of the task and the ways of working at it.[3]

Among the many kinds of "unwilling" clients are parents who have been reported as neglecting or abusing their children. This is a peculiarly difficult situation for the interviewer, who cannot tell the parents who made the accusations. One suggestion is that before seeing the clients, the interviewer should have as much contact as possible with the source of the report in an effort to evaluate the severity of the problem. If the situation appears to be urgent, a home visit without notification may have to be made promptly; if it is less urgent, a telephone call or a letter might do. There is no easy way to arrange this first interview, and no one has found a perfect solution. Interviewers have to deal with their own ambivalence toward what seems an invasion of privacy, and also have to overcome any tendency to become a partisan of either the informant or the client. A friendly but fairly reserved calmness is usually desirable both in talking with the informant and with the clients. Once the interviewer has made contact with the clients, skirting the issue of the nature of the problem will only delay matters; openness on this subject is generally the best policy to follow in such situations.

There also are families who—on the surface at least—do not want help. Often impulsive in their behavior, often in trouble, often faced with a multitude of problems, often known to a number of agencies, they are hard to help and hard to engage in using services profitably. Endless patience is required, and many efforts to reach out are necessary.[4]

There is another kind of situation in which clients may or may not be "willing." In institutional settings (medical and psychiatric facilities, children's institutions, correctional settings), clients are in a sense captive. Here the worker's authority is derived from the authority of persons in the setting: doctors, corrections officers, administrators. Ambulatory clients may be reluctant to come to an interview, but they are required to come; the bedridden patients have to stay in bed. Clients may withdraw from the interview by maintaining silence or feigning sleep. If the social worker's services are completely optional, such defenses against intrusion are unnecessary and clients can verbally communicate a decision not to continue contact. In any case, it is up to the worker to explain the nature of the services available and (when applicable) the source of the referral and the reasons for it. The client may then move toward being a "willing" client.

There are a few things that workers can avoid doing: they can avoid starting with a preconceived idea of what the world looks like to these clients; they can avoid assuming that denial of the problem means that they feel no discomfort; they can avoid taking sides (with them or against them) in order not to play into a continuing and fruitless battle; and they can avoid lecturing—these clients already have been objects of exhortation and this has not helped them. What workers can do in a positive sense is to start with the observed reality that somebody thinks the clients are in trouble. How has this come about? Why do they suppose they have been forced into the position of client? What is their perception of the circumstances that led to this? How do they feel about the people who have made them talk to a social worker? What do they think the worker's power over them might be? What do they expect the worker and agency to do to them?

At this early point in the interchange it may well be that the only discomfort that such clients can acknowledge is the discomfort of having somebody else say that they have a problem. Recognition of their own part in the problem (if this exists) and a definition of the problem may come much later and may be the end result of the worker's helping efforts. In situations such as this the rules of interviewing are applied in a context that differs markedly from the earlier example, but the rules still hold.

Individual Interviews in the Beginning Phase of Work with Groups

This discussion has focused on offering help to individuals and taking the first steps toward establishing a contract. In work with groups, the development of goals takes place in the context of the group, but separate interviews related to this purpose are sometimes useful. There may be individual interviews to help clarify what the clients expect from the group, what they can bring to the group, and what the experience might have to offer them and ask of them. Persons entering a group—whether an established group or one in the process of formation—may have both fears and hopes that need to be recognized and understood. Are they joining friends or strangers? Do they wonder what the other members are like? Do they wonder what the group will think of them? How do they see themselves in relation to the stated purpose of the group?

A beginning exploration of such questions in individual interviews has several purposes: it helps prospective group members become aware of their own feelings, it moves them toward a realistic perception of the group and of themselves in relation to it, and it gives them an experience with the worker as a helping person and future resource.

Notes

1. I am indebted to Genevieve Oxley, who has developed the idea of "wide open," "focusing," "narrowing," and "closed" questions much more fully in her teaching materials. Also see the examples set forth in David R. Evans, Margaret T. Hearn, Max R. Uhlmann, and Allen E. Ivey, *Essential Interviewing* (Monterey, Calif.: Brooks/Cole Publishing Co., 1979).

2. General goals of service are stated in the various definitions of practice at a fairly high level of abstraction. At the other extreme, detailed and specific goals often are described in case reports. Goals are implied—and sometimes specified—in the literature on diagnosis and treatment. For an overall consideration of goals, see the general references cited in the bibliography (Compton and Galaway, Hamilton, Hollis, Keith-Lucas, Perlman, and Smalley). In addition, note the following articles: Werner Gottlieb and Joe H. Stanley, "Mutual Goals or Goal-Setting in Casework," *Social Casework*, Vol. 43 (October 1967), pp. 471- 81; Julianna T. Schmidt, "The Use of Purpose in Casework Practice," *Social Work*, Vol. 14 (January 1969), pp. 77- 84; and Anthony N. Maluccio and Wilma D. Marlow, "The Case for the Contract," *Social Work*, Vol. 19 (January 1974), pp. 28- 37.

3. See Chapter 4 for a fuller discussion of the client's sense of powerlessness. Also see Genevieve Oxley, "Promoting Competence in Involuntary Clients," in *Promoting Competence in Clients*, ed. Anthony N. Maluccio (New York: The Free Press, 1981).

4. Sally Holmes, Carol Barnhart, Lucille Cantoni, and Eva Reymer, "Working with the Parent in Child Abuse Cases," *Social Casework*, Vol. 56 (January 1975), pp. 3-12. A few additional articles also are suggested: Kenneth Dick and Lydia J. Strnad, "The Multi-Problem Family and Problems of Service," *Social Casework*, Vol. 39 (June 1958), pp. 349-55; Ruth Ellen Lindenberg, "Hard to Reach: Client or Casework Agency?" *Social Work*, Vol. 3 (October 1958), pp. 23-29; Alice Overton, "Serving Families Who Don't Want Help," *Social Casework*, Vol. 34 (July 1953), pp. 305-309; Robert Sunley, "New Dimensions in Reaching-Out Casework," *Social Work*, Vol. 13 (April 1968), pp. 64- 74; and A. Selig, "The Myth of the Multi-Problem Family," *American Journal of Orthopsychiatry*, Vol. 46 (July 1976), pp. 526- 41.

Chapter

3

Some Common Concerns of Interviewers

Dress and Behavior

Beginning interviewers often are concerned about their personal appearance and behavior during an interview. The one clear guideline for workers is that the way they look and act should not impose an obstacle to communication with the client. This means that interviewers should have some regard for the conventions of the place where they are working and the expectations of the clients. If workers flout agency conventions, their ability to work with colleagues will be reduced, and this in turn will reduce their opportunity to give maximum service to the client. If they ignore the client's expectations, they will impose a barrier between themselves and the client.

For example, a young woman was assigned to work with a group of elderly conservative Mexican women. When she prepared to go into the field she was wearing a sleeveless, short-skirted dress, but fortunately the supervisor (herself a Chicana and thoroughly familiar with the traditions) noticed this in time and explained how shocking the costume would seem to the group the worker wanted to help. The worker should take into account clients' perceptions of what is appropriate dress and behavior for a professional person.

In most agencies, casual clothes are customary, but there are exceptions. Even now there is at least one hospital in Southern California where men are required to wear a jacket and tie. Conventions vary over time and in different settings and geographical areas. Common sense suggests that interviewers find out what the conventions are at the moment. This does not mean that they have to give up all their individuality or be entirely colorless, but it does mean that they sometimes will need to make a compromise between their personal taste and the preferences of both agency and clientele.

The physical behavior of interviewers should indicate interest in and concern for their clients' welfare. It seems fairly obvious that if they lean back and close their eyes, fidget with things on their desk, carry on a telephone conversation, or gaze steadily out the window, they are withdrawing from their clients. Touching is another matter. To hold a crying child is completely natural, but to embrace a weeping adult is of questionable value—but tissues should be kept available: for one thing they are needed, for another this conveys the message that other grown people also cry. The hand clasp or touch on the shoulder in farewell should be sensitively timed; such touching may make some clients feel that the interviewer cares about them, but could make others shy away in discomfort. It is impossible to give precise instructions about body language. In general, interviewers should maintain some eye contact, but not stare; should lean toward clients, not away from them; and should show responsiveness by facial expression as well as words.

Use of First Names

Another question concerns the use of first names between client and interviewer. Again, conventions differ. In many

groupwork settings the use of first names long has been an accepted practice. Among social acquaintances and business associates it is common practice to reach a first-name basis almost immediately. This is less true in the relationship between patient and
doctor, client and lawyer, or student and teacher. There is something to be said for the formality of the use of last names between
client and worker, since this emphasizes the professional rather
than the social nature of the relationship. This is, nevertheless,
in large part a matter of personal taste and the particular requirements of the situation. An illustration from community organization practice points up some of the problematic aspects in the use
of first names:

> A new white worker going into a Black neighborhood as-
> sociation meeting heard other people using first names, and
> wanting to be "one of the boys" also started using first
> names. A distinct coolness developed very rapidly. When he
> mentioned this to his supervisor he was reminded that
> many of these people were recent migrants from a part of
> the South where no white man ever addressed a Black man
> as "mister." Former workers had used the title "mister"
> until invited to address members on a first-name basis. The
> worker, by failing to recognize the symbolism of his act,
> had performed in a way that underlined the group's basic
> mistrust of white people in positions of leadership.[1]

Even when problems of this kind do not exist, it is not
acceptable to call adult clients by their first names and expect
them to address the interviewer with the formality of the last
name, since this implies that the worker is in the position of an
adult, and the clients are in the position of dependent children.
An exception to this rule exists in some settings where use of
clients' first names provides a degree of anonymity.

Gifts

What does one do about gifts and greeting cards? Clients
often are moved to bring the interviewer a gift of some sort. With
adult clients this most often happens at the point of termination,
and usually an appreciative acceptance is all that is indicated. It
should be noted, however, that in some public agencies there are
strict rules that prevent the worker from accepting any gifts from
a client, and such rules of course must be observed. When bringing
gifts becomes a ritual, or when gifts are obviously far more expen-

sive than the client can afford, the interviewer should discuss the matter with the client and refuse to accept the gift.

The groupworker faces a special problem in maintaining a sense of professional purpose within the informal atmosphere of the group. The parting gift to the worker could be acknowledged with pleasure and appreciation, and some such comment as: "I'll think of you and remember you, and the gift also will remind me of all that you accomplished this year."

Most agencies that work extensively with children make provision for giving birthday and Christmas gifts, and sometimes gifts on other occasions. These are gifts from the agency, although the child sees them as personal gifts from the interviewer. Such provision is made because candy, treats, and gifts are to children the tangible evidence that the adult cares about them. Birthday cards and other greeting cards are important to children because they are evidence that even when absent, the interviewer still thinks about them.

Personal Questions and Comments

The worker often is faced with personal questions and comments from the client. These are sometimes not easy to deal with and may be of particular concern to the beginning interviewer. Such personal questions and comments stem from several motivations, the most prominent of which are the following:

1. Simple social curiosity—an attempt to "place" the worker in the general scheme of things.
2. An attempt to find out what the worker's qualifications are and what characteristics will be helpful.
3. An attempt to control the relationship, to make it a personal friendship that will hold the worker permanently, or to make the relationship personal in order to avoid the problematic aspects of the professional relationship.
4. An expression of feeling about the worker.
5. An expression of feeling about the client.

Unless a question arises in an unusual context, or unless a question is one that is usually not considered socially acceptable, a brief and straightforward response with no comment about the possible meaning of the question is usually the best procedure. Such questions as: "Are you married?" "What does your husband (or wife) do?" "What part of the country do you come from?" can usually be handled in this way. What the interviewer needs to remember here is that although clients have some curiosity about the person they are talking to, they are far more concerned about themselves and the problems they are facing, than they are about the worker and the worker's problems.

Some questions are quite directly asked in order to determine the worker's qualifications. "What kind of education did you have for this job?" "How much experience have you had in this work?" These are obviously attempts to assess the interviewer's professional competence. They are particularly hard questions to respond to for the student and the beginning interviewer. An honest answer may cause the beginner some embarrassment, but a false answer simply will lead to greater trouble. The interviewer may be tempted to explain too much, to exaggerate a limited experience, or to apologize for a lack of full qualifications. Such responses tend to increase the clients' concerns rather than to mitigate them.

One way of dealing with this sort of situation would be similar to the following: "I have had some courses in college." Or, "I'm working toward my master's degree in social work now." Or, "The agency has a special training course that I have taken." If this does not suffice, the interviewer might ask: "Does this bother you?" Or, "Are you afraid I can't help you?" It is rare that clients make any further issue of the matter. Usually the beginning interviewer's intense desire to help comes through strongly and is in itself a helpful measure.

Questions also may center on a client's concern about the worker's personal qualifications. It is as if the client were saying: "How can a young girl understand the problems that I am facing now that I am old and retired and sick?" "How can a woman who has never been a mother understand what it is like to bring up children?" "How can an unmarried boy have any idea of what it means to have problems in marriage?" "How can anybody over 30 understand what it's like to be 16?" "How can a person like that with a steady job have any idea of what it is like to be poor?" Sometimes the client's questions suggest these meanings and sometimes the client will say in so many words: "You cannot possibly understand what I am going through because you have not been married and you have not had a sick child."

It is not convincing for workers to pretend to have a knowledge or experience that they do not possess. Even if they *have* been married and *have* had a sick child, their experience of these events inevitably will have been different from the client's. Thus interviewers must guard against the assumption that the client's reactions will be the same as theirs. When a client asks a question about the interviewer's age, for example, and the interviewer is reasonably certain that this really is a question about qualifications, the interviewer might respond: "It sounds as if you think I am too young to understand what you are going through." Any such comment should be phrased rather tentatively and questioningly so that the interviewer's impression can be easily corrected by the client if need be. If the interviewer's hunch is confirmed and the question does have to do with qualifications for understanding, it might be recognized openly with the client that the worker has not had similar experiences and thus the worker's understanding may be limited by this. All that interviewers can do is try to understand what the client is feeling so that they can be of maximum help.

If, on the other hand, the interviewer's experiences have been similar to those of the client, the interviewer still needs to express an awareness that despite similarity of experiences, there may be a good deal of difference in the way people react to these experiences, and it is the client's way of dealing with events that is important. The purpose of any of these procedures is to keep the focus on the client's situation and feeling about it, rather than shifting to the worker's situation and the worker's feelings, which are not of primary interest to the client.

Another possible meaning of personal questions and comments from the client is that they may represent an attempt to develop a friendly relationship which can be the basis of a lifelong mutually gratifying and mutually demanding connection. This is a tempting situation for the interviewer. It often happens that client and interviewer share many tastes and interests and develop a strong mutual affection. There is some difference of opinion about the extent to which a personal friendship can be allowed to develop without impinging on the quality of help the interviewer can offer to the client.

The author's advice is to avoid a personal friendship, at least during the period when the client is making use of the interviewer as a professional helper. The reason for this is that the double demands of a professional and a personal relationship are very difficult to meet. An attempt to carry both roles easily can result in ambiguities and misunderstandings that could reduce either the quality of the professional relationship or the quality of the friendship. Friendship may become partisanship, and partisanship reduces objectivity. If interviewers have some conviction about this, they can explain it to the client in so many words without insult or injury. The client's repeated attempts to make the interview a social occasion, repeated invitations to dinner, or suggestions for mutual excursions can be dealt with quite directly in this way. The worker can say: "I know you would like this to be a personal friendship and I am sure you realize that I genuinely like you. But I know that I will be able to see things more clearly and help you better if we don't try to make a social friendship out of this. I also think you will be freer to talk about the things that are troubling you."

Personal questions and comments may represent—directly or indirectly—clients' feelings about the worker or clients' feelings about themselves. Unless these are persistent and are interfering with the progress of the interview, they require little response from the worker. For example: "Where do you buy your clothes?" can represent admiration for the worker's appearance, a desire to be like the worker, envy that the worker can afford better clothes, or even deprecation of the worker's appearance. The simplest thing to do is answer the question factually. If this behavior persists, the worker may have to make an active intervention: "It seems to me you have made an awful lot of comments about my appearance, and I am wondering how this is connected to what we are discussing."

Occasionally personal comments identify the worker with someone else who was important in the client's life. When a woman client says: "You remind me a lot of my father—the way you talk and the way you look," there are several ways that an interviewer could respond. The client's comment could be ignored either on the basis that it was irrelevant to the problem at hand or on the basis that any exploration would be too emotionally loaded to be profitable at this time, or the interviewer simply could wait receptively to see whether the client wanted to talk further about her reactions or whether this was a way of beginning to talk about her father and what he meant to her in relation to the development of the present situation. Also, on the basis of the interviewer's knowledge about the client, active exploration of either the client's feeling about her father or about the interviewer could be undertaken.

There are a number of things related to the exchange of personal information in the interview that are sometimes problematic. Should workers give their home telephone and address in response to the client's question? There is no clear-cut answer to this. Some interviewers working with certain types of clients find that this information serves as reassurance that the worker is truly concerned about the client and wants to be available to give help if an emergency arises. In dealing with other kinds of clients, however (people who tend to act out, the insatiably demanding client, and some of the mentally ill), interviewers may be inundated with excessive telephone calls or visits, or contacts that carry the threat of personal danger. An appropriate decision requires considerable judgment, and the situation often is difficult to assess. It is obviously safer to avoid giving one's address and telephone number, and some agencies have explicit rules about this that must be observed.[2]

Notes

1. This example from practice was suggested by Eleanor Ryder, formerly a member of the Council on Social Work Education staff.

2. There is another school of thought that urges "self-disclosure" as evidence of a worker's genuineness. Gerard Egan, though making the stipulation that content and timing of any sharing of the worker's own life experiences should be only in the context of what might be helpful to the client, makes a strong case for self-disclosure. He also believes that the relationship between interviewer and client should be completely "role-free." It seems to me that at best, self-disclosure is superfluous, and that at worst, it meets the worker's needs at the expense of the client's. Also, I cannot envision a relationship between a person asking for help and a person offering it that does not have some differentiation of roles. The major part of Egan's book, however, is extremely useful in learning something about interviewing. See *The Skilled Helper* (Monterey, Calif.: Brooks/Cole Publishing Co., 1975).

Chapter
4

Reactions of Client and Worker to the Helping Situation

The questions discussed in the preceding chapter arise at many different points in the course of the contact between client and worker. We will return now to the early phase of the helping process and to some of the things that vitally affect the content of the interviews.

Clients' Options in Selecting Services

Do clients have any options about their contact with the social worker? In the example given earlier (the elderly man seeking financial help), the client presumably was making application of his own volition. But what choices does he actually have if he is in financial need and does not have extensive resources within his own family? He probably has no alternative except to make application to a public agency. He has no choice about which agency this will be, nor does he have any choice about which worker he will see. In other kinds of applications (such as those related to placement of children, planning for the use of medical care, or for counseling or psychotherapy) the range of choice may be somewhat wider. It is nevertheless narrow for the person who does not have ample financial resources. In general, the less money a person has, the fewer the options, and even in voluntary agencies, social workers are likely to see clients whose choices are limited because of financial constraints.

This lack of opportunity of choice is more conspicuous in some agencies than in others. People in child care institutions or in medical and psychiatric settings may be offered services that they are free to reject, but sometimes the institution imposes the requirement that the client see a social worker. In correctional institutions and in probation and parole this requirement is present. In protective services, where society has concern for the neglected or abused child, social work services are imposed on the parents.

These realistic limitations on the range of the client's choice constitute a dilemma for social workers who are committed to the idea of self-determination as a positive value.[1] This is why the means of giving help are important. Because social workers value the capacity to make responsible decisions and because clients usually have already experienced some restriction in the range of decisions they can make, it is important to support whatever decision-making power the client does possess and to open up new possibilities for exercising this capacity. To the extent that interviewers manipulate clients, they are depriving them of the chance to exercise their capacity for choice.

Clients' Sense of Powerlessness

Because this problem of clients' freedom or restriction in making choices affects their attitude toward the worker and the content of the interview itself, it deserves further examination. It already has been pointed out that limited financial resources effectively reduce the options available to clients in seeking service. The implications of the familiar saying, "Beggars can't be choosers," are distinctly disparaging. Although clients may not be beggars in the literal sense and simply may be claiming that which is their right, they may well translate the phrase in their own minds to, "People who cannot choose are beggars and therefore are not worthwhile."

This is almost self-evident when the client's request has to do with financial assistance or personal services that most people pay for themselves. When the worker has some degree of discretion in giving or withholding financial assistance or in determining its amount, the control that the agency exercises over an important part of the client's life appears to be vested in one person.

The sense of powerlessness and of being subject to another person's control is not limited to situations in which the client is asking for financial help. Persons with ample financial resources who seek medical care may have genuine freedom of choice in selecting a physician. Once they have placed themselves in a physician's hands, however, the amount of control they have over the situation becomes limited. The more serious the illness and the more frightening the symptoms, the more completely the patient feels a loss of control. The physician has access to a body of knowledge and to medical resources that the patient does not possess. While patients may feel the need of the physician's authoritative knowledge, they also may react in a seemingly irrational manner to the fact of their dependence on the doctor.

Individual members of the counseling groups in correctional settings and mental hospitals may share this feeling of powerlessness, especially when they are under some compulsion to join the group. In other forms of groupwork, the view of the helping situation is frequently different. When group members have an effective choice in their use of the social worker, they may feel freer to communicate their dissatisfaction.

In any helping situation, then, some degree of power or control is inherent in the role of the helping person.[2] In some social work situations the amount of this control is so trivial that it has no effect on the relationship between the worker and the client, but in some cases it is a central problem. Its potential importance is such that one must be alert to its effect both on the client and the worker. When the client's reaction appears to be excessively submissive, passive, angry, or suspicious (and any of these excessive reactions may impede the giving of help), one must first consider the reality of the present situation. Has the worker in fact done something to arouse such a response, or has the agency's reception of the client caused it? What kind of treatment has the client experienced in the waiting room? Has the client had to wait an unreasonable length of time before seeing the worker? Was the waiting room crowded and uncomfortable? Did the receptionist treat the client discourteously? Has the worker failed to give full attention to the client? Has the worker misunderstood the client's request or made unwarranted assumptions about the nature of the request? Has the worker been abrupt or inquisitorial in questioning? If any of these things has occurred, it is generally wise to acknowledge it frankly and attempt to get the interview onto a more productive basis.

The worker might say something like: "I know you have had a long and uncomfortable wait and I don't blame you for being annoyed about it. Let's see what we can do now that we have some time together." Or, "I think I have been asking too many questions and I don't really understand what it is that is worrying you most at this time. Let's see if we can start over." Comments of this kind, like other activities of the worker during the interview, are based on some sort of hypothesis about the nature of the difficulty the client is experiencing and its causes. Such an hypothesis is supported or refuted by the client's response to the worker's comments. If a simple effort of this kind results in a more productive participation on the part of the client, then there is no need to seek more elaborate explanations.

Sometimes there is no apparent reason in the immediate situation for the client's reaction, or if there is such a reason the worker's effort to restructure the situation is unsuccessful. The reason for the client's behavior may lie in a prior experience with this agency or with others, or perhaps in things that the client has heard about the agency from other sources. If the experience with the worker is favorable, the client's distrust, anger, or passivity should diminish. It also is possible that the client's experience in being dependent on or controlled by other persons in the environment either currently or in the past may have affected the response to the present situation.

Although workers should be sensitive to any evidence emerging in the course of the interview, they ordinarily would not suggest such explanations verbally in a first interview and might not even make an attempt to explore the reasons for the client's behavior at this point. Only if the inverview becomes completely unproductive would such exploration appear to be indicated. Even then the worker's "interpretation" should take the form of a tentative question rather than an assertion.

Interviewers' Feelings About Their Role

Interviewers' feelings about their role in the helping situation as well toward a particular client or group of clients also will affect the progress of the interview. It is easy enough to specify some of the attitudes generally believed to enhance the possibility of clients telling their own story and taking appropriate action in relation to their problems: acceptance of clients as persons, respect for their rights, expressions of interest and concern, objectivity, empathy, recognition of clients' values, and avoidance of imposing personal moral judgments.

The conscious motivation for entering the field of social work is a liking for people and a desire to help them. The fact remains, however, that clients are not equally likeable nor are they equally receptive to helping efforts. Workers, in their efforts to treat all clients equally and fairly, may conceal from themselves differences in their feelings toward different persons. When we are unaware of these feelings, we do not have conscious control of their expression; if the feelings are strong, they find expression in devious ways and may constitute an impediment for the client. The feelings themselves are not to be feared. Workers who are fully aware of the complicated mixture of positive and negative feelings that they have toward particular individuals have a much better chance of managing their expression of feeling in such a way that it can be used for the benefit of the client rather than in a damaging way.

Workers should become alert to strong feelings within themselves about the particular client when signs of tension appear and when there is some deviation in their usual way of operating: for example, a prolonged preoccupation with an interview that has been completed; a feeling of confusion about what was going on in the interview; delay in arranging for an appointment or failure to meet an appointment on time; a sense of extreme gratification about clever management of an interview; a tendency to prolong the interview beyond the usual time span; an impulse to arrange for special interviews; a desire to do things for and with the client outside of agency practice; a tendency to take sides with the client against other members of the family or against the agency; a ritualistic adherence to the rule book; a marked change in the level of activity during an interview such as suddenly becoming much more passive or much more active in conversation with the client; an unaccustomed sense of apprehension or anticipation in advance of an interview; a feeling of pleasure in the client's dependence (which can be very seductive); a reluctance to transfer the client to another worker or to another agency when this is indicated; a continuation of services beyond the point where they normally would be terminated. These are examples of the signs that point toward some kind of emotional involvement with the client.

Often the feelings that prompt this behavior are essentially positive in the sense of an overidentification with the client and an intense desire to be of maximum help. Workers have to sort out these feelings and begin to understand them. This is a job to be undertaken without imposing the problem on the client. When workers understand the personal meaning of their anger toward the rejecting parent or their intense wish to give adequate parenting to the neglected child, it becomes apparent that their underlying emotional needs cannot be gratified realistically through the client, and it then becomes much easier to handle the feelings that have been engendered. It becomes possible for workers to focus once again on the person who is asking for help rather than on their own needs.

A somewhat more subtle and perhaps pervasive difficulty is involved in workers' perceptions of themselves in the helping role. Their feelings about controlling and being controlled, about exercising power over another, or having power exercised over them will come to light. Workers who long for dependency may seek gratification by making others dependent on them. Workers who see the power and control of the helping person as a potentially fearful thing may react to it by denying the control that they must exert. In an effort not to impose idiosyncratic values on the client, they may act as if they have no moral standards whatever. To the extent that reactions such as these distort the reality of the situation in which the worker and client find themselves, they become an obstacle to productive interviewing.

Workers' Responsibilities in Their Relationships with Clients

For interviewers, reflection on all of these matters usually takes place outside the interview. By thinking these things through, interviewers are in the process of changing themselves so that they have different equipment in their own personality and reactions that they can offer to the client in a spontaneous way. With experience in interviewing and with a steady increase in self-awareness, they become better able within the interview itself to understand their own feelings and to avoid a detrimental use of them. Such mastery is in itself a legitimate source of pleasure and gratification. It makes it possible for interviewers to watch with satisfaction the client's increasing independence and eventual separation from them.

The emotions that client and worker bring to the interview are important determinants of the quality of the relationship that develops. Although there are variations in the degree to which different theorists assign a place to the relationship as a central aspect of the helping process, all schools of thought agree that in order to be helped the client needs to have some sense of trust in the worker. Workers cannot create this sense in the client nor should they assume that this is their responsibility. What they are responsible for is the management of their own feelings and an awareness of their impact in arousing certain responses in the client. The client is, however, a feeling and thinking human being separate from the worker and influenced by innumerable life experiences other than the relationship with the worker. It is unrealistic for workers to imagine that they have full control of the interaction between themselves and the client and that they can manage this relationship in its entirety. It is my view that an accurate understanding of the relationship at all points in the contact with the client is an important aid to understanding the interchange between the persons concerned and in reducing the apparent confusion of an interview to manageable proportions.

Notes

1. The classic reference on self-determination is the article by Felix P. Biesteck, "The Principle of Client Self-Determination," *Social Casework*, Vol. 32 (November 1951), pp. 369-375. Also see Saul Bernstein, "Self-Determination: King or Citizen in the Realm of Values?" *Social Work*, Vol. 5 (January 1960), pp. 3-8; and Alen Keith-Lucas, "A Critique of the Principle of Client Self-Determination," *Social Work*, Vol. 8 (July 1963), pp. 66-71.

2. In connection with this and the subsequent discussion, see two articles by Elliot Studt: "An Outline for Study of Social Authority Factors in Casework," *Social Casework*, Vol. 35 (June 1954), pp. 231-38; and "Worker-Client Authority Relationships in Social Work," *Social Work*, Vol. 4 (January 1959), pp. 18-28. Also see J.P. Kahn, "Attitudes Toward Recipients of Public Assistance," *Social Casework*, Vol. 36 (October 1955), pp. 359-65; and Robert K. Taylor, "The Social Control Function in Casework," *Social Casework*, Vol. 39 (January 1958), pp. 17-21.

Chapter

5

Topics Covered in Initial Interviews

So far we have considered some of the elements that affect the content of initial interviews: the nature of the problems presented, the context in which they occurred, the clients' feelings about the problems, their reactions to the workers, and the workers' feelings about the particular client and about their role as helping persons.

Are there certain topics that always must be covered during the early part of the contact? It is clear that an understanding of what clients want from the agency and what they think it is that the agency is going to offer them is of primary importance. This is true in all the practice methods. The following discussion, however, relates primarily to work with individuals and families.

General Guidelines

It seems logical to suppose that if the agency is going to offer help there should be some understanding of the ways in which clients have already tried to solve the problem and the kinds of resources that are available to them, either their own or from within their immediate environment. In the course of such an inquiry it is hard to imagine a situation in which it would not be relevant to know something about the members of the family, the state of their health, the housing situation, the financial resources, the occupation and employment of the various members of the family, and their vocational and educational preparation.

Depending on the nature of the problem and the kind of help that the agency can offer, a detailed consideration of the present situation in respect to some of these factors may be indicated; in some instances past history may be important. These general topics are quite natural for clients to mention in describing their situation, and usually the worker's disciplined expression of interest is sufficient to elicit a rough picture.

Checklists and Outline Forms

Agencies with specialized functions often give the worker (or in some instances the clients) a check list or form to be filled out, or a highly structured series of questions that must be asked of the clients. A clearly delineated structure of this sort has certain advantages, but also presents some hazards. If the form is appropriate to the problem in hand, it can be helpful to clients in reviewing relevant information. This in itself may give clients some perspective on the problem and increase their awareness of their own resources for dealing with it; it may help them clarify the nature of the problem and the nature of the request. For workers, the sense of ambiguity about what should be covered is reduced. When the form has been completed, workers may feel some confidence that they have done their job adequately — a confidence that is sometimes unwarranted.

Problems in Using Prescribed Forms

The trouble with a prescribed form rigidly used is that it can distort the problem that the client wants to present. When an agency develops a detailed interview outline or application form it is with the idea that all the important information about any client who comes to the agency should be covered. Thus some of the questions may be irrelevant to a particular situation and others may be inadequately developed. If one gives equal weight to every question, the client's picture of the situation may be obscured. A form neatly completed or an extensive history obtained by following precise rules is probably no more than a monument to conscientious effort. A dynamic picture of the problem as the client sees it, the circumstances surrounding its onset, the nature of the client's motivation for change, the resources within the client and the client's immediate associates for dealing with the problem, and the nature of the client's expectations of the agency still may be missing.

Sometimes merely asking particular questions will suggest to the client that an affirmative answer will make it more certain that the agency's services will be offered. For example, in state mental hospitals it is often part of a social worker's routine assignment to obtain a social history from the relatives of a patient who is to be admitted. Questions about convulsive seizures or drinking habits may lead relatives to exaggerate the evidence or even invent it if they are anxious to have the patient admitted to or kept in the hospital, and they think that a positive response will guarantee this objective. On the other hand, if relatives are anxious to have the patient discharged, they may tend to minimize the evidence. In order to assess the accuracy of the history given by relatives, the worker needs to understand their motivation. Then an explanation of the uses to which the history will be put may enable the client or the relatives to give a more accurate picture of the whole problem situation.

Creative Use of Forms

An interview outline can be used creatively and for the benefit of the client if its main outline is relevant to the situation and if the worker has some conviction about its relevance that can be conveyed to the client both explicitly and implicitly. When clients are talking freely and openly about their problem situation, it is unlikely that they will be following an outline as specified in an interviewer's schedule. Nevertheless, they probably will touch on most of the topics that need to be covered. They may move back and forth between the several topics and may elaborate on some of them at considerable length. If workers have the major topics firmly in mind, they will — almost without knowing it — express interest as the client begins to touch upon these subjects. This interest may be shown by a change of posture, an inquiring look, a murmur of question or assent, a brief question to clarify what the client is saying ("Did this happen after Lucy left home?" or "This happened just after you were married in 1977?"), a comment about the client's feelings ("It sounds as if you were pretty upset about that." "That was a pretty hard time for the family I guess."), or a direct suggestion that the client tell more about a particular event.

When the major topics of the interview schedule or outline have been covered in this way, the interviewer can then return to the form and ask supplementary questions if these are necessary. It is a good idea to review with clients the main outlines of the story, particularly when the account has been rambling or complicated. This will give interviewers a chance to verify their own perceptions of what the client has said, and it will give the client an opportunity to correct any errors.[1]

My experience has been that the kind of procedure outlined above is generally effective. There are, however, variations in interviewing style, and some of these variations may be equally effective. Some workers prefer to begin the interview by taking down a few essential facts: this gives clients a chance to hear the tone of voice of the interviewer and to begin to hear the sound of their own voice, and this may help them start talking. The interviewer can then move to a less-structured phase and the procedure may continue in a manner similar to that already suggested.

When the client is talking somewhat repetitiously (and this can occur in early interviews as well as later ones) it becomes more difficult for interviewers to follow the basic rules. They may find that their attention is wandering and that they are not giving their full mind to what the client is saying; and when interviewers fail to give the client their full attention, they may unwittingly jump to conclusions and assume that they understand what is meant, when actually they should be asking for clarification. Why is the client repeating material that has already been discussed? Is there something new in the present account? Does the client perhaps think that the interviewer did not hear the first time? Is the client so lost in memory of a situation that it is impossible to move beyond the past? Has the interviewer somehow suggested that this material is of special interest and therefore a constant repetition of it is somehow gratifying? Interviewers cannot assume that they know the answers to these questions; they must give the client their full attention, avoid jumping to conclusions, and ask for clarification when necessary.

Note-Taking During Interviews

Beginning interviewers frequently are concerned about taking notes during the interview. Nobody would expect the interviewer to remember accurately such things as street numbers, exact dates, and other factual data. To write down such things in the presence of the client and to verify their accuracy is a businesslike procedure. The situation is different when clients are talking freely and sometimes rapidly about their circumstances and the problems that they face. Some workers find that they are so worried about trying to remember what the client says that they feel more comfortable in the interview and better able to pay attention to what is going on if they occasionally jot down a few words to remind themselves of the content of the interview at a later point.

Note-taking, however, may have the unfortunate effect of distracting the worker from what clients are saying or even distracting them from what it is that they want to say. Clients may begin to feel some concern about just what it is the worker is writing down. Extensive note-taking during an interview is usually unnecessary. Only at points of confusion, when the worker wants to verify with a client certain complicated relationships or clarify a confused series of events, is it necessary to review the facts with the client and jot them down.

The general guideline is this: interviewers should follow a procedure that does the least to interfere with their attention to what clients are saying and to the feelings they are expressing about the events they are recounting. Further, interviewers should follow a procedure that gives clients some confidence that they are making a serious attempt to understand accurately what they are being told. In some instances this may require writing things down; in other instances it requires a kind of direct face-to-face attention undistracted by paper and pencil. When the focus of the interview is on present emotions and on the interaction between worker and client, then note-taking would seem entirely inappropriate.

This consideration of checklists, prescribed forms, and note-taking leads directly to the problems of record-keeping and confidentiality that will be discussed in the next chapter.

Note

1. For a survey of the historical development of the social study and the variations in its use related to theory, see Carel B. Germain, "Social Study: Past and Future," *Social Casework*, Vol. 49 (July 1968), pp. 403-409. An earlier article by Emilie T. Strauss suggests the values of exploring employment history as a means of understanding the client's problems: "The Caseworker Deals with Employment Problems," *Social Casework*, Vol. 32 (November 1951), pp. 388-92. A classic from the psychiatric literature is John C. Whitehorn, "Guide to Interviewing and Clinical Personality Study," *Archives of Neurology and Psychiatry*, Vol. 52 (September 1944), pp. 197-216.

Chapter
6

Recording and Confidentiality

Interviewers are required to keep some sort of record of who has been served, the service that has been offered, and the outcome of this service. Traditionally, such a record "belongs" to the agency, and the agency is supposed to protect the record in the interest of the client. This is not as simple as it sounds. The issues of what should be written down, who should have access to it, and the extent to which confidentiality can be preserved are by no means resolved.[1]

Purposes Served by Agency Records

Records are absolutely essential for administrative purposes. Statistical reporting is directly related to the survival of the agency and its services: it is the basis for funding, for substantiation of staff needs, and for program planning. No matter who compiles the statistics, it is the worker who supplies the basic information about who received what services, and over what period of time. This is the information the administrator must have in order to know whether the agency's purposes are being carried out. Is the agency reaching the population it should reach? Should some of its programs be expanded or reduced? Should new approaches be attempted? Are staff assignments reasonably equitable?

In some agencies, records are necessary to qualify for third-party payments (such as Medicare), and also are needed for quality control and peer review. The purposes of recording that are more immediately visible to the worker are those of providing continuity of service, communicating with other professional persons in the agency who also are working with the client or the family, and providing a base for supervisory discussion and review. Records to be used in teaching or research usually have to be specially prepared if they are to be effective.

Who Has Access to the Record?

It is apparent that the worker is not the only person who sees the record. Confidentiality in this sense is a myth. What can interviewers promise? They can assure clients that their situation will be discussed only with colleagues who have special expertise in matters relating to the particular circumstances, and they also can say that the client's permission will be sought before information is shared with persons outside the agency.

All of this seems obvious, but it takes considerable vigilance to live up to these promises; interviewers are interested in their job and in their clients, and they find it difficult not to talk in a casual way about the situations that absorb so much of their working time. Every safeguard should be employed to ensure that information about the client is used responsibly. This may necessitate discussion with a colleague, the supervisor, a consultant, or other members of the staff who are concerned with helping the client. In many cases, the issue of confidentiality does not arise and it is not necessary for the interviewer to bring it up; the interviewer conveys a responsible attitude toward the client in many small ways and not just by guaranteeing secrecy. But when the clients preface a remark by saying that no one else in the world should know about this and they do not want it to go "into the record," then the worker must in all honesty specify the limits of confidentiality that can be observed.

Once a piece of information is in writing, the interviewer no longer has full control over it. Agencies may make serious attempts to keep their records confidential, but the files are available to persons working in the agency, and the information thus can be obtained by clerical staff and others who are not directly concerned with helping the client. Agency files have been subpoenaed by the courts, and the privileged nature of the communication between social worker and client is by no means assured. It is a safe rule for interviewers to write the record in such terms that they would be willing to have the client read it. Since passage of the 1974 Freedom of Information Act, it has become essential that clients have access to information about themselves that is in the record or stored in a computer or on tape.

The use of case records for teaching raises another issue of confidentiality. It long has been customary for schools of social work to obtain agency permission before using a written record, well-disguised, for classroom purposes. With the increasing use of tapes and videotapes, it also is becoming more common to get the client's direct permission. It is customary for the client to have an opportunity to listen to the tapes or to view the videotapes before granting such permission. A written record should be subject to the same conditions. A blanket consent form, once so commonly used, is not sufficient; a separate consent form should be obtained every time a release of information is requested, and the client should know the content of the material released.

If interviewers shudder at the thought of having the client read the record, they should take a good look at what they have written to determine what material they would rather not have the client see. For instance, have derogatory or gossipy comments been made about the client? Or about fellow workers? Or about the agency? Or about other agencies? Has a diagnostic label been used that is beyond the interviewer's expertise? Has information been included that has not been shared with the client? Has speculation been stated as fact? Has highly incriminating information been included that is not absolutely essential?[2]

These questions suggest that there are some restrictions on what interviewers write and how records are kept. If they are working separately with two members of a family who are at odds with each other, it may be wise to maintain separate records. The very nature of some agencies in such fields as adoptions, child placement, psychiatric settings, and corrections will pose special problems. Administrators and the agency's legal consultants need to be informed fully about the implications of record keeping in case of a lawsuit. To keep no records is not the answer: such a course leaves the agency open to the charge of irresponsible practice.

The political implications of group members' activity pose a different order of problem to the community organization worker. Here confidentiality can be extremely important. Workers need to be ready to help individuals protect themselves against revealing to workers or to the organization matters that really are not their business. Workers also need to help them develop ways to protect themselves from an invasion of their right to organize.

For example, in one city there was a community council to which residents of the area could belong if they paid the $2.00 membership fee. This was during the McCarthy era and one of the women members, a card-carrying Communist, was arrested for inciting to riot in a demonstration. When asked for identification of the organization that she represented, she showed her membership card from the community council. Subsequently, the president of the community council came to the worker for help because the city postmaster had asked for a list of names of members of the council who worked in the postal department.

An example from groupwork practice suggests another common problem related to confidentiality. In street-corner work an individual member of the group might come to a worker to give "secret" information that there is going to be a gang fight that night. The "secret" may be told with the implicit hope that the worker will intervene. In any case, workers in this situation would be obliged to clarify their stand and the interventive action they might propose to take.

In all forms of social work practice there are occasions for making explicit the nature of confidentiality and its limits. It is better for clients to keep certain information to themselves than for them to experience betrayal of a promise.

Use of Records as a Helping Measure

The use of audiotapes and videotapes for research and teaching has led to the discovery that playing back the recording to the client had some therapeutic uses not recognized earlier.[3]

Such a playback may be used in the interview itself. It gives clients a chance to see and hear themselves in ways that had perhaps not previously been available to them. They thus may get a new perspective on their behavior and this may be a subject for further discussion. The written record rarely has been used in this way and its potentials are quite different. The written material is a distillation of the worker's perceptions of the client and the situation. Clients reading the case record would not be seeing themselves in action, but would be seeing someone else's perception of them. Any device that increases the possibility of a mutuality of perception of the situation and what can be done about it would be worth trying.

Types of Social Agency Records

This is not the place for extensive discussion of the form of social agency records, but because interviewers always have some responsibility for record keeping, a description of various types of records is in order. Records may be short or long; they may be kept in a card file or in a folder; they may be kept for a brief period of time or may be preserved in the agency's files almost indefinitely. The variations ideally should be related to the agency's purposes and the particular problems of the clientele, but the traditions of an organization sometime become so entrenched that certain formalities are adhered to even though their utility is no longer apparent. The general tendency is to reduce the length of recordings and to maintain minimal records. Virtually all agencies keep some sort of card file that identifies the client and indicates the period during which services were given. Usually the card file includes the reasons for the application and the reason for closing. Beyond this, agency practice varies considerably. It is common practice to maintain a folder in which are filed the face sheet and application form (which includes identifying information and such factual information as addresses, telephone numbers, birthdates, marriage dates, etc.), some sort of record of the interviews held and the services offered, and copies of correspondence with the client or on behalf of the client. There also may be various documents signed by the client authorizing specific activity on the part of the agency and its staff.

That part of a social agency record which deals with the interviews themselves may take a number of different forms:

1. A social history covering specific topics (See Chapter 5).
2. "Process recording" of all interviews or of selected interviews (discussed below).
3. Summaries at specified periods with an indication of the dates of the interviews that are covered and statement of the major developments during this time.
4. A summary that is included at some turning point in the situation.
5. Detailed or brief opening and closing statements including an indication of the dates of interviews and the persons involved.
6. A summary at the point of transfer.
7. A summary prepared for the purpose of psychiatric consultation or other consultation or prepared for staff discussion.

Methods of Recording

Methods of recording include longhand, typing, dictating, taping, and videotaping the actual interviews. The first three methods (of which longhand is the most time-consuming) all require that the worker first think through the content and organize it. Taping and videotaping require no such prior thought. Both have their uses in teaching, supervision, and (as noted earlier) in helping the client. But an hour's taped interview takes an hour to listen to and is not useful as a permanent record; transcription of a taped interview takes many hours of clerical time and results in a very bulky record — again, not useful as a permanent record. If tapes are used, the interviewer still must organize the content and put it in an abbreviated form.

Process recording is commonly required of students for some or all interviews. The process record is not a verbatim report, but it includes considerable detail about the content of the interview and the sequence in which the discussion occurred; it also includes the worker's comments on the kind of emotion displayed by the client and the client's general behavior and appearance, as well as the worker's reactions to the interview. The process record is an enormously important method of teaching oneself, and it also may be a useful tool as a basis for supervisory or consultative help to the interviewer. The act of recalling and writing down the events of the interview almost forces one into an analysis of one's own activity. Even the most experienced interviewers will find it helpful to engage in such analysis when they have completed interviews that for some reason puzzle them or leave them with the uneasy feeling that they have somehow missed the meaning. This process of reflection and analysis may reveal to interviewers feelings of their own that they were not aware of during the interview but that interfered with their perceptions of clients and their responses to them. There are a few social agencies that regularly require process recording of all interviews, but this pattern is becoming quite rare. The process record is chiefly valuable to the interviewer and does not have a place in the agency's permanent file. The briefer forms listed above will serve the agency's purposes more effectively.

Notes

1. Suanna J. Wilson, *Confidentiality in Social Work: Issues and Principles* (New York: The Free Press, 1978); and *Recording* (New York: The Free Press, 1980). Both books include a practical exposition of the problems and ways of dealing with them; both have an extensive bibliography.

2. Wilson, *Recording, op. cit.*, pp. 189-202.

3. Evidence of the value of the playback is discussed by Ian Alger and Peter Hogan, "Enduring Effects of Videotape Playback Experience on Family and Marital Relationships," *American Journal of Orthopsychiatry*, Vol. 39 (January 1969), pp. 86-98. Also see Ida Oswald and Suzanne Wilson, *This Bag is Not a Toy: A Handbook for the Use of Videorecording in Education for the Professions* (New York: Council on Social Work Education, 1971).

Chapter

7

Some Common Obstacles to Mutual Understanding

It has been suggested earlier that the method of disciplined attention is usually effective in eliciting history and in covering major topics of concern in an application interview. But there are times when the procedures previously delineated do not work. There are a number of obstacles to communication that occur, whether or not differences in race and associated differences in culture also are present (to be discussed in Chapter 8).

Physical and Mental Problems

There are some conditions under which a productive interview is impossible: when clients are suffering from extreme physical exhaustion, when they are heavily sedated, when they are

under the influence of other drugs, or when they have been drinking heavily. There also are severe limits on the kind of communication one can have with a person who is severely mentally retarded
or who is in an acute stage of mental illness. All these obstacles to
communication are a matter of degree. In their milder manifestations they affect the quality of the interview, but do not prevent
some sort of productive interaction between worker and client.
The worker needs to be alert to the possibility that a client who is
having difficulty in presenting a coherent story may be handicapped by one of these physical or mental states.

Blindness, deafness, and speech handicaps pose other
kinds of problems in interviewing. Under ordinary circumstances
we are dependent on vision for a good deal of our communication.
Blind clients depend on hearing and feeling to understand their
environment.[1] They resent being shouted at or treated as if they
were mentally as well as physically handicapped. Oral communication with the blind is easily possible, but these persons cannot
pick up the visual clues that are so important a part of ordinary
conversation. It is helpful to tell such clients briefly and factually
anything they may need to know, such as the location of the ash-
tray or telephone if either is to be used. There is a fine line between being overly helpful and being insufficiently helpful.

The hearing-impaired (who depend much more heavily
on their sight) also resent being shouted at. Even if they are not
expert lip readers, they will be able to understand the interviewer
more easily if they can see the interviewer's face clearly. Interviewers should avoid covering their mouth with a hand or murmur-
ing in an undertone. Reasonably clear enunciation without much
raising of the voice may be adequate to permit the client to understand, as long as the interview room is quiet.

The plight of the totally deaf is far more serious. Some
are highly skilled lip readers and also can speak (though their
speech may not be understood easily). Many communicate freely
only in sign language, which has a structure of its own, and they
need an interpreter in order to exchange complex ideas. Writing
is always a possibility, but is very laborious. Nevertheless, I think
it is important for interviewers to communicate as directly as
possible, and with the fewest possible intermediaries between
themselves and the client. The deaf are cut off from society in
ways that the hearing world (including persons with a hearing
impairment) can scarcely visualize: they have extremely limited
access to higher education, they cannot use an ordinary telephone,

and radio and most TV programs are unavailable to them. The well-educated and talented have difficulty finding employment that makes use of their abilities. Hence my conviction is that contact with the hearing world should be encouraged whenever possible. Obviously, with both the blind and the deaf, the worker needs to be particularly alert to the points at which the client has misunderstood what is said.

Speech handicaps present a different kind of problem for the client. Stutterers may have to talk very slowly; they are desperately in need of the worker's patience in hearing them out. There are various neurological disorders that can affect the rate of speech and the kind of pronunciation the client uses. Surgery involving the trachea or the vocal cords may make it impossible for clients to talk in an ordinary voice and in some cases may make it impossible for them to make themselves understood even in a whisper. The interviewer has to watch a tendency to talk in the same way that the client does, or to put words into the client's mouth when the client is having difficulty forming words.

All the physical and mental states mentioned above and all the handicaps noted may impose a good deal of strain on the client and make the interview fatiguing. This should be taken into account in planning the length of the interview. Clients may not feel free to say that they are too tired to go on but workers should be aware of signs of fatigue and should propose an early termination if this seems indicated. Even when clients have an illness or handicap so severe that they are virtually unable to communicate with the worker, one should never assume that they are oblivious to what is going on. They should never be treated as if they were unconscious objects unable to perceive their surroundings.

Differences in the Use of English

Those of us for whom English is our native language do not always share a set of words and phrases that are mutually comprehensible. Difficulties range from a simple misinterpretation of some of the words being used to a total mutual misunderstanding. Worker and client may have a different vocabulary or they may ascribe different meanings to words that they both use.

First, let us consider possible differences in the use of words. Regional accents and regional use of words vary so radically from Texas to Maine and from Oregon to Louisiana that a stranger to the region is sometimes hard put to understand directions to the local post office. Given the mobility of our population, it is not unusual for a client to encounter a worker whose whole way of speaking is almost foreign. In one locality the term "falling-out" means some form of epileptic seizure or temporary loss of consciousness; the same term elsewhere means a disagreement or a quarrel. In addition to such regional idiosyncrasies, there are specialized vocabularies among gangs, prisoners, drug users, and other subgroups. Slang usage differs in relation to locality and also changes rapidly over a period of time. Words that were once considered obscene and are still considered improper by many groups of people are increasingly accepted as a part of normal conversation among others. Interviewers cannot take it for granted that they understand the meaning of all the words the client uses or that they understand the emotional implications of a term; nor is it safe to assume that the client fully understands the worker's English.

The worker frequently needs to take active steps in order to overcome these obstacles to mutual understanding. Much of this is done in direct contact with the client, and the simplest thing to do is to ask direct questions. For example: "What happened when there was this falling-out?" Or, "I am not sure I know what you mean by that word." Sometimes professional people or volunteers who are working with particular groups in a community can be helpful in clarifying a specialized vocabulary. Professional literature, case studies, and fiction also provide some clues. Sometimes the client's reaction during the course of an interview signals a lack of comprehension of what the worker has said. Among the signals are the look of incomprehension, the irrelevant response, or a kind of passive acceptance or denial which to the client may seem to be what the worker is seeking even though the client has not quite understood the question. At such points it may be useful to rephrase the comment or question, or ask the client whether the question or comment has been understood.

Some interviewers consider it important that the worker use the same colloquial and specialized vocabulary that the client uses. In the author's opinion, a self-conscious effort to make use of such a vocabulary introduces a note of artificiality that defeats the purpose of the interview. Inaccurate use of slang or of a specialized vocabulary reveals the falsity. It is a safe rule for workers to use ordinary language that comes naturally to them. At the same time, they should avoid the use of technical or professional terms that may seem colorless or even meaningless to the client.

For example, social workers tend to use the term "hostility" to cover a wide range of emotions from irritation to extreme rage. To be mildly irked by an event is not the same thing as to be furiously angry. The point is that workers should choose a vocabulary that accurately reflects their meaning in terms that are comprehensible to the client.[2]

Ways of Living

Another possible source of misunderstanding lies in the unspoken differences that client and worker may have in their perception of a way of life and the ways that social institutions affect their way of life. Many of us take it for granted that parents are protective and that family life has a degree of predictability to it. Family members sit down around the same table to eat. There are regularities about when meals are served, where each person sleeps, times of getting up and going to bed, and times when family members go to school or to work or undertake other tasks. This picture may have nothing to do with the events in clients' lives or with their idea of how a family should be organized.

When a mother complains that her young son does not eat well or that he does not go to school on time or that she cannot get him up in the morning, the interviewer cannot take it for granted that these difficulties are occuring in the context of the regularities that have been described. It behooves the interviewer to make specific inquiries about the nature of family routines in order to understand the background in which disturbing events occur. In some families the members rarely share a common meal. The individual family member eats when spurred by hunger and eats what can be found. There may be no regularity about where or when each person sleeps. Parents may not be protective, and children may have an unrealistic degree of responsibility for themselves. When there are no adult, employed members of the family, the schedule imposed by the necessity of going to work is not present, and this may make it more difficult to introduce regularities related to going to school.

Such patterns of family living are often found in lower-class, poverty-stricken groups. At the same time, one cannot assume that this stereotyped picture of irregularity is always found among the poor. Interviewers have to keep in mind the possibility that family patterns in the client's situation may differ markedly from their own family patterns. If most of their clients come from the same neighborhood or the same ethnic group, they gradually will become familiar with the common standards and expectations. Even then, of course, they must keep their minds open to the individual variations and the differences among families.

Views of Family Structure, Sex Roles, and Sexual Behavior

There are some curiously contradictory trends in current ideas about family structure, the "proper" roles of men and women, and "proper" sexual behavior. This means that interviewers need to be aware of their own prejudices, preferences, and stereotypes if they are to be helpful to those clients whose attitudes differ markedly.

The legally sanctioned marriage with life-long fidelity between the partners, and with the male as sole breadwinner and the female as a homemaker, wife, and mother is a pattern of living that has never been accurately descriptive of all couples, and is now being challenged by many. Communal living, sexual freedom outside marriage, serial mating, bisexual relationships, temporary or life-long partnerships between members of the same sex — all these variants are openly espoused by some and condemned by others.[3] The right to contraception and legal abortion are religious and political issues. The battle over equal rights for women is emotionally loaded, with all its implications of wider career opportunities, increased self-assertion, and greater sexual freedom.

The people who come to social agencies asking for help in family relationships are sometimes living in conventional patterns, and sometimes in alternative arrangements. Freedom from the legal ties of marriage and parenthood does not mean freedom from problems in relationships. If interviewers are to be useful to people whose ideas of family structure and sexual behavior differ strongly from their own, they will need to know what their own standards are (have they just taken them for granted?) and examine carefully their own reaction to the client's standards. If they fail to do this, they easily can fall into the trap of attributing all the client's difficulties to "overly restricted" or "overly free" behavior, instead of being able to perceive major problems that are only tangentially (if at all) related to sexual behavior. If interviewers are shocked by certain behavior, they should take a good look at the basis of this sense of shock. Is it because the behavior is illegal? Hurtful to others? Or perhaps because it represents a fantasy of their own?

I do not suggest that workers should give up their standards. There may be times when it is appropriate to express them in so many words. A bland mask of acceptance can be perceived by the client as a failure to be genuine and honest. But it is one thing to say: "I can't really go along with this; have you thought of what is happening to the children?" and quite another to say, "What you are doing is immoral." In the first instance, workers would be indicating that though their standards differed, they were trying to stimulate the client's thinking about the possible consequences of particular actions. In the second instance, workers could be closing off any further exploration.

While little is known about the ways in which the sex of worker and client affect the interview,[4] it seems possible that it could be a force retarding or promoting communication at least in the initial phase. But many other variables — not just the gender of worker and client — enter into the picture. Some clients react to an interviewer — regardless of sex — as either maternal or paternal. Some make what seem to be deliberate attempts to shock the worker by at once revealing unconventional sexual behavior or using exceptionally colorful street language. Such attempts ordinarily disappear in a short time. But sometimes the introduction of bizarre sexual fantasies is a sign of more serious emotional disturbance. Workers should trust their own feelings to the extent that when the client's talk gives them a "creepy" feeling, they should seek the best consultation they can find.

Views of Social Institutions

How do clients view such institutions as the school, the police, the courts, or the health department? Some people see them as essentially supportive and protective. Others, however, perceive them as far from benign, and may approach all social institutions with an attitude of distrust and provocativeness. If the school appears to be a custodial institution that deprives them of freedom and offers no real opportunity, motivation for getting an education will be reduced. If the courts and the police are seen as arbitrary oppressors rather than as protectors, then they are to be avoided or outwitted. Such attitudes of distrust may carry over into all relationships with constituted authorities, even when the person representing the social institution is making a genuine effort to be fair.

The worker needs to understand the individual's perception of these various social institutions and any previous experience with them. This helps to explain the ways in which the client is currently using, or failing to use, available opportunities. Furthermore, some of the attitudes that the client has toward representatives of social institutions may be directed toward the worker. This can happen regardless of the worker's race. To the client, the worker represents the establishment, and as such, may be the object of the client's distrust. Such attitudes are never easy to handle.

When workers are putting forth their very best effort to help a client, it is disconcerting to be greeted with anger and distrust, and it is all too easy to respond with an expression of hurt and a wish to retaliate. With some self-control it is possible to present at least an appearance of neutrality in the face of such attitudes on the part of the client, and in the beginning of a contact this is probably as effective a form of behavior as anything else. However, if the distrust does not subside sufficiently so that the client can make use of the help the worker is offering, it will sooner or later be necessary to face the problem openly. Sometimes this can be done quite simply with such a comment as: "I know you don't really trust me in this situation. I wish you would at least try it out for a little while to find out whether I mean what I say." Sometimes a more extensive discussion will be necessary. The worker might comment on other experiences the client has had: "I get the impression you have had difficulty several times with the welfare department and with the people at the school. Maybe you think I am going to be just the same."

Values

Differences in values often are associated with social class. Typically, middle-class values place a high priority on working, saving, and planning for the future, whereas lower-class values place a high priority on taking and consuming in the present. This highly simplified description of extremes does not fit all individuals. One finds both planfulness and impulsivity at all economic levels. Note, however, that a person who is living above the poverty level has some economic margin for impulsivity in buying or spending, whereas the person who is living at the poverty level or below has no such margin. Hence, when the person on a relief budget spends five dollars for liquor, some essential expenditure for food, clothing, or housing is reduced; but when a person living above the poverty line makes a similar purchase, no serious inroads are made on the resources available for essential items.

This is something for interviewers to remember when they are moved to condemn the client for what appears to be a foolish expenditure. It is far easier to plan for the future and to postpone gratification when there is a good reason to hope that gratification will occur in the future, than when one's whole experience has been that gratification is withheld and should be grasped whenever it is available.

A number of studies have indicated that there are social class differences in what people expect of a counselor in social agencies or psychiatric clinics. There is some evidence (not fully confirmed) that working-class and lower-class clients value more direct activity from the worker in terms of advice or specific helping measures. Talking about emotions and trying to understand their own behavior and feelings may seem quite irrelevant to them. Middle-class clients, on the other hand, are more likely to see talking as a useful method of helping. Again, there are wide individual variations. What is important here is that the interviewer try to find out what it is that the client expects, and how these expectations relate to the services that the worker is able to offer. This process is part of the development of the original contract between worker and client and often requires reexamination at a later point. Clients who want information and advice may be unwilling to invest themselves in a series of interviews that are aimed at developing their self-awareness.[5]

Notes

1. Hector Chevigny and Sydell Braverman, *The Adjustment of the Blind* (New Haven, Conn.: Yale University Press, 1950). See particularly the references to lay attitudes toward the blind as part of the social environment in which they must live. This book, despite its focus on problems of the blind, suggests the areas to which one must be sensitive in working with people who have other handicaps.

2. Two articles by John D. Cormican include an extensive discussion of these problems. See "Linguistic Subcultures and Social Work Practice," *Social Casework*, Vol. 57 (November 1976), pp. 589-92; and "Linguistic Issues in Interviewing," *Social Casework*, Vol. 59 (March 1978), pp. 145-51.

3. See, for example, Marny Hall, "Lesbian Families: Cultural and Clinical Issues," *Social Work*, Vol. 23 (September 1978), pp. 380-85; and Helen A. Mendes, "Counter-transference and Counter-Culture Clients," *Social Casework*, Vol. 58 (March 1977), pp. 159-63.

4. Mary C. Schwartz, "Importance of the Sex of the Worker and Client," *Social Work*, Vol. 19 (March 1974), pp. 177-86; and Julia B. Rauch, "Gender as a Factor in Practice," *Social Work*, Vol. 23 (September 1978), pp. 388-95. Rauch's article includes an extensive bibliography.

5. Allison Davis, *Social-Class Influences Upon Learning* (Cambridge: Harvard University Press, 1950). Also see Elizabeth Herzog's review of the literature and her questioning of some popular assumptions in "Some Assumptions about the Poor," *Social Service Review*, Vol. 37 (December 1963), pp. 389-402; H. Aronson and Betty Overall, "Treatment Expectations of Patients in Two Social Classes," *Social Work*, Vol. 11 (January 1966), pp. 35-41; and John E. Mayer and Noel Timms, *The Client Speaks* (London: Routledge and Kegan Paul, 1977). The evidence of class differences in preference for "action" rather than "talk" is not fully confirmed. Harold Graff, Lana Kenig, and Geoffrey Radoff, reporting on a study of 50 lower-class patients in a psychiatric hospital, found no confirmation of the idea that lower-class patients see all things as involving action rather than internalized processes. See "Prejudice and Upper-Class Therapists Against Lower-Class Patients," *Psychiatric Quarterly*, Vol. 45 (1971), pp. 475-89.

Chapter

8

Racial and Associated Cultural Differences as Obstacles to Mutual Understanding

Would a reasonably observant Black interviewer expect all Blacks to look alike? Think alike? Behave in the same way? I doubt it, just as I doubt that white interviewers would have such expectations of other whites, Koreans of other Koreans, and so on down the long list of groups of people whom we think of as belonging to different races.

The term "race" is imprecise; it often is used interchangeably with "nation" and "people" to "designate one of a number of great divisions of mankind, each made up of an aggregate of persons who are thought of, or think of themselves as comprising a distinct unit. In technical discriminations, all more or less controversial and often lending themselves to great popular misunderstanding or misuse, RACE is anthropological and ethnological in force, usually implying a distinct physical type and certain unchanging characteristics, as a particular color skin or shape of skull."[1] Despite the imprecision of this definition, there is no question about the strength of feeling that racial differences arouse and the detrimental effects on society that occur as a result of the discrimination, deprivation, and animosity that exist. Discrimination is sometimes quite subtle, but in the long run is damaging. What is referred to here is that form of deprecation of potential capacity manifesting itself in reduced expectations of a person. If a child is not expected to do well in school and is not expected to be "college material," the chances are that the child will live up to those expectations and will not exceed them.

Stereotypes

The interviewer, employed in an agency that offers services to individuals, is usually faced with the necessity of working with clients of different races. Somehow the inherent obstacles to communication must be sufficiently overcome so that the task at hand can be accomplished. I am making certain assumptions here: that the interviewer is a person of good will who wants to understand the difficulty the client is facing and wants to be helpful. But good will is not enough. In order to move beyond good will, interviewers need to be aware of the stereotyped picture they hold of persons of their own and other races, examine these stereotypes in relation to available facts, and discover how they have developed and how they are maintained.

Have you ever heard somebody say: "I'm not a racist, but . . ." or "Some of my best friends are . . ." Look behind these words (spoken by another, or spoken or thought by yourself) and you will find traces of the racism that affects us all: a stereotyped picture that interferes with our perceptions of the unique human being whom we want to help.

Not all stereotypes are pejorative, though some carry a derogatory implication. Many are false and many are based on scanty evidence, but all are demeaning in the sense that they are oversimplified. A few examples come to mind: "Asian Americans are a 'model' minority who take care of their own and have few problems" (research indicates that this picture is false). "American Indians are lazy" (the cultural value of patience may be misinterpreted as laziness). "Blacks are naturally musical" (well, some are). "Unmarried mothers (and the speaker is usually referring to members of racial groups other than the speaker's own) have more illegitimate children in order to get a larger relief check" (there is no evidence for this proposition). The list could be extended, but these few examples indicate the importance of searching for facts rather than relying on popular assumptions.

Sources of General Information

One can learn a good deal from books about the general social characteristics of the various racial groups in the United States: their origins, the circumstances that brought them here, distribution of age, sex, marital status, typical size of families, predominant religious beliefs, the roles of the family members, customary methods of solving problems or of seeking help, levels of education, employment patterns, income levels, and many other facts relevant to understanding the influences affecting individuals.

The most easily accessible summaries of such general information will be found in the *Encyclopedia of Social Work*,[2] which contains a series of articles on minorities filling over 50 pages. In addition to a lengthy introductory article, there are separate papers on American Indians, Asian Americans (including Chinese, Japanese, Koreans, Thais, Vietnamese, Guamanians, Hawaiians, Filipinos, and Samoans), Blacks, Chicanos, Puerto Ricans, and white ethnics. There are no separate articles on groups from Central and South America or from Cuba, nor is there mention of the recent immigration of Jews from Russia or of the many Iranian students whose status here is equivocal. Jews, despite the fact that they are numerically a minority and have a long history of persecution and discrimination, are mentioned only parenthetically as one group of "white ethnics." Source material for these articles includes census data (with its widely publicized undercount of minorities in central cities), some excellent surveys of particular groups in a given locality, and extensive other sociological and historical studies. As one looks at this long list, one also should consider that within most racial groups there are disagreements on methods of achieving an improved condition.

All of us came here from somewhere else. Bronowski postulated that the Indian tribes of North and South America came from Asia at a time when the Bering Straits formed a land bridge during the last Ice Age,[3] but the reason for this migration is unknown. The late-comers, including all the other groups enumerated in the *Encyclopedia,* left their homelands for a variety of reasons: in search of conquest, wealth, adventure; in search of political and religious freedom; to escape hunger; to escape persecution; or to find a better life. Some arrived as indentured servants, and some were imported and sold as slaves. Others, already occupying the land (such as the American Indians, and some of the Chicanos of the Southwest), became part of the population of the United States by virtue of conquest, land purchase, or treaties. This hasty sketch is offered only as a reminder that the problems of minorities and of the waves of immigration are not new.

The amount of space given to minorities in the 1977 *Encyclopedia* is in sharp contrast to the five pages allotted to this subject in the 1965 edition. The change reflects a new form of census data (which at the time the 1965 edition was prepared did not include information on the composition of the nonwhite population), the liberalization of immigration laws, and the increased emphasis on positive racial and cultural identity by the various groups.

Sources of Information about Interviewing Minorities

A careful study of the section on minorities in the 1977 *Encyclopedia* may leave one feeling ignorant, confused, or overwhelmed. Until about 1970 there was almost no social work literature that dealt with the problems of crossracial, crossclass, or crosscultural interviewing, except in relation to Blacks and whites. Since then there has been some increase in journal articles that deal with these matters. As far as I know, there is no one volume that brings together the available knowledge in this field. The appended bibliography contains many references to Black-white interviewing (including the collection of articles edited by Goodman[4]), as well as a few concerning American Indians and some about interviewing Chicanos, Puerto Ricans, and other Spanish-speaking groups. There are a number of special issues of social work journals (from the 1970s) that focus on single racial groups, though for the most part these deal with major social problems rather than with interviewing.

The emphasis on large social issues is understandable in view of the severity of the problems of employment, education, health care, and housing. But when specific services are to be provided to individuals, we still must find ways of communicating, one by one, across the barriers of race and the barriers of cultural differences that often attend racial differences.

Given the diversity of races and the diversity that exists within each group, it is too much to expect that any one interviewer can be equally competent in working with all groups. (This is quite aside from the problem of language differences, which will be discussed later. I am assuming for the moment that interviewer and client have enough common vocabulary to carry on a reasonably coherent conversation about the problem at hand.) If a large proportion of the persons interviewed are from one or two races or nationalities other than the interviewer's, the interviewer will need to be informed as fully as possible about the experiences and customs that affect most of the members of such groups.

How can interviewers acquire this essential knowledge? In the long run, their clients will educate them, but since the clients have come to them to obtain a service and cannot be expected to concentrate on teaching them, they will need to learn from other sources. This is a large task, but not everything has to be learned at once. Interviewers probably will start by using what is most quickly available. There may be persons in the agency who can be helpful, persons who (because of their knowledge of the local situation) can offer specific guidelines; but it is desirable to use more than one source, since each may reflect some idiosyncratic bias. Books are useful. Interviewers should read everything they can, not just the social work literature (starting with the *Encyclopedia*) but also history, biography, and fiction.[5]

Publications of this kind will help give the interviewer a general picture, but the local situation may well differ materially; sometimes, too, conclusions drawn from an excellent study in one geographic area are inappropriately applied to all areas. Furthermore, there is a time lag between data-gathering and publication. Thus it is particularly important that interviewers be aware of what is going on in their own community. Other available resources are such things as newspaper articles and Letters to the Editor, TV programs, and theatrical, musical, and dance performances. In most large cities, the Yellow Pages of the telephone book include a long list of social agencies with services for a specific racial minority, and workers in those agencies can be a good source of information.

Finally, interviewers should take note of the people they see: on the bus, going to school, in supermarkets, in department stores, and in restaurants. I do *not* suggest an inquisitive stroll in an inner-city center of poverty — that would be asking for trouble. But I would urge that interviewers increase their perceptions by using all available means.

Some Elements to which the Interviewer Should Be Attentive

There are a number of things to which interviewers especially should pay attention. The list that follows is not a questionnaire: its purpose is to help interviewers become sensitive to some of the elements that may, to a greater or lesser degree, affect their clients' lives, their clients' way of dealing with difficult situations, or their clients' way of behaving toward them in the interview.

1. Under what circumstances did the the client's group become part of the population of the United States? (By conquest? By treaty and land purchase? Imported as slaves? Imported as cheap labor? Excluded from another country? Seeking refuge from intolerable physical or political situations elsewhere? Looking for an opportunity to better their lives economically?)

2. Is the client an immigrant? Or of the second or third generation? If the client is an immigrant, when was the date of arrival? The country of origin is important, but it is also relevant to know whether the person comes from an urban or rural area. China, for example, is a very large country with a wide range of climates, many different spoken languages, and sharp differences between remote rural areas and large cities. The older Chinese may never have learned English, while the second or third generation may be bilingual and may have been well-educated in American schools. There are generational gaps based partly on the time of immigration and partly on the degree to which the younger generations accept or reject customs valued by their elders.

3. Is the client's life largely segregated from the rest of society? Such segregation has the strongly negative

factor of cutting the client off from other important cultures, but in some instances has the strength of a closely knit group with accessible mutual aid of either an organized or highly informal nature.

4. If the client is an immigrant, to what extent has immigration affected potential employment opportunities and social status? It is likely that there has been some reduction in status, though this is not always true. In the case of well-educated, recently arrived Chinese, Japanese, Koreans, and Filipinos, language handicaps are a serious obstacle to regaining the employment status they experienced before immigration.

5. What are the customary family roles among the client's group? Is there a clearly defined role for father, mother, children, or extended family members? Interviewers should remember that their client's experience may not fit the picture they have received reading sociological studies. A Puerto Rican woman, for example, was irritated by an interviewer's assumption that all Puerto Rican men were macho and all women subservient.

6. If the clients are Chicano, Black, or American Indian, interviewers can expect that the group will have experienced discrimination, humiliation, poverty, poor housing, poor health care, poor education, poor nutrition, and poor employment opportunities. But the individual's experience may have been less-damaging, or even more-damaging, than that of the group as a whole.

7. What are the culturally determined attitudes toward time? The idea of scheduled appointments, punctually kept, and lasting for a specified period is unknown to some cultures, whereas it is fully acceptable to most persons in Northern European and North American industrialized nations. It is difficult to operate a large program efficiently without some system of scheduling interviews, but it is possible. Emergency services (such as suicide prevention agencies, many medical settings, and Travelers Aid) regularly function on a loose schedule. One result, of course, is that some clients have to wait to be seen;

but this may be preferable to a rigid structure of
appointments. Some groups are unprepared to
plunge directly into a business-like interview, but
are more likely to be responsive if time is allowed
for a leisurely beginning with a fairly lengthy exchange of courtesies and small talk. If interviewers
move too fast in their efforts to focus on the client's
problem they probably will get nowhere. It is hard
to gauge when the leisurely beginning represents a
pattern of avoidance, and when it is a necessary pre-
liminary to a serious discussion. Experience with a
cultural group and sensitivity to individuals will
help interviewers make reasonably accurate judgments. The pace of the interview (the rapidity of
speech and response) is governed partly by cultural
factors, but also could be affected by the extent to
which the client *thinks* in English. For some who are
able to understand and speak English fairly well,
responses may be slow because they are mentally
translating the interviewer's words into their own
language, thinking of the response in this language,
and then translating it back into English. Give them
time! The interviewer also should remember that it
is not necessary to speak loudly to a person whose
English is somewhat limited, but it *is* necessary to
speak slowly, to be alert to signs of incomprehension, and to rephrase comments or questions that
may not have been understood.

8. What are the usual ways in which the client's group
prefers to deal with the problems of finding a job,
finding a place to live, getting medical care, resolving
family disputes, or coping with interpersonal and
emotional difficulties? There is evidence that public
resources are underutilized by many minority groups
because of a lack of knowledge about them, because
they are not readily accessible geographically, or
because the modes of helping are culturally uncon-
genial. Although there is considerable variation
among minorities, many rely first on friends and the
extended family, and prefer to seek help through
their own ethnic group. For many, to seek outside
help with personal problems would be extremely

distasteful.[6] Thus the interviewer's well-meant effort to be helpful will meet with rejection unless there is an understanding of what kind of help will be acceptable within the client's culture.

9. What is the characteristic body-language within the cultural group? The conventional white American interviewer may be baffled when clients avoid any direct eye contact, when they respond with a smile to almost any comment, when they gesticulate violently, when they either maintain great physical distance from the interviewer or approach very closely, when they talk very loudly or talk in a faint monotone. It is a mistake to assume that any of these aspects of behavior is necessarily a sign that something is wrong. In some cultures, direct eye contact is a sign of disrespect; similarly, facial expression, physical distance, gesticulation, and tone of voice may be culturally determined.

This listing takes account only of some of the rather broad racial and cultural factors that affect the individual with whom the interviewer is talking. Differences in social class within each group have not been mentioned, but they exist. Some observers believe that the common interests of members of the same race are much more powerful than the common interests of members of the same social class who come from different races.

Can the Gap Be Bridged by 'Matching' Interviewer and Client?

Given the complexity of communication between races, even when interviewer and client both speak English with reasonable comfort, what is the best way of bridging the gap? Should Black clients be interviewed only by Black workers? Whites by whites? American Indians by American Indians? Chicanos by Chicanos? Matching of this kind is a practical possibility when an agency is set up to serve only one group and is staffed entirely by members of the same group. It is difficult, if not impossible, when both clientele and staff are multiracial. Even if matching is considered desirable, the availability of minority interviewers with specialized education is extremely limited. An alternative is to use indigenous paraprofessionals and provide in-service training and professional supervision.

The evidence for matching and for the use of para-professionals is equivocal. While many authors believe that it is easier for an interviewer to make contact with the client if both are of the same race and social class, some research on Black clients and both Black and white interviewers indicates that the higher the competence of the interviewers, the less important is their race.[7] Kadushin[8] suggested that some Black clients feel that if they are assigned to Black workers, they are getting "second best"; and some feel that Black workers are less understanding because they have become identified with the white, middle-class professional. Nevertheless, the mix of Black and white may provoke some irrational responses and some deliberate needling of the white worker, and there are situations in which it is almost imperative that worker and client be of the same race.

Under the most benign circumstances, interviewers must deal with considerable anger covertly or openly expressed; and with the increasing militancy of many minority groups, the white worker faces enormous hostility.[9] Silverstein, in recounting her experiences as a white worker in a racially mixed ghetto (with Black, Chicano, and white residents), spoke of the intergroup conflicts and the distrust, hostility, and manipulative behavior she had to face.[10] In this instance it seems doubtful that a Black or Chicano worker could have survived any more easily. Cross, however, made a strong case for having an all-Black staff in an institution for Black delinquent girls. She believed that only the person who had experienced what it means to be Black could make contact with girls whose main job had been survival.[11]

In working with Chicanos, Medina and Reyes commented on the special problems that they (as Chicanas themselves) had encountered.[12] Clients have difficulty in accepting a woman as a professional. The Chicana counselors, as well as their clients, are under pressure from their minority group to live by old Mexican norms — a countertraditional-cultural dilemma for both.

An experimental study by Santa Cruz and Hepworth involved Mexican-American and Anglo or Germanic clients assigned to workers of the same or other race. The authors concluded that the clients' perceptions of the quality of their relationship with the worker was not based on similarity in cultural orientation, but rather, the worker's competence was the determinant.[13]

Both color-blindness and ethnocentricity can cause problems. Cooper commented that an overbalanced stress on ethnicity can obscure individual differences.[14] Among a number of case examples, she cited a situation in which a Chinese client was seen by a Chinese worker in a psychiatric clinic. The worker focused on the client's problems of cultural identity, though it eventually became clear that the client's real fears had to do with his own possible homosexuality.

Attneuve, and Lewis and Ho commented on the difficulty faced by non-Indians in gaining the confidence of their clients.[15] They all, however, called attention to tribal differences and individual variations within the tribe. Lewis and Ho suggested that Native Americans who have devalued their own culture cannot be good social workers with any tribe. The articles cited are valuable because of their analysis of tribal networks and some common value orientations, as well as their warnings against stereotyping.

It seems fairly obvious that matching, of itself, does not solve all problems. The Black interviewer, for example, is faced with as many difficulties in communicating with a Black client as the white interviewer is in communicating with a white client. There is a further argument against matching. In a large agency with a multiracial staff and a multiracial clientele, it could well be that certain workers have developed special skills in dealing with a particular type of problem. If one of these specialists is Black, should the white client be deprived of that specialist's skill?

What Can Be Done When Worker and Client Have No Common Language?

The discussion so far concerns people of different races and cultures who nevertheless can use English as a means of communication. If the client speaks and understands absolutely no English, and the worker has little or no command of the client's language, alternative arrangements must be made. The only truly satisfactory solution is to have bilingual and bicultural professionally educated interviewers, an ideal that is far from realization in 1982. At present, such well-equipped interviewers are rare, and are likely to be sought after as executives and teachers.

There are several other possibilities:

1. *Use of an interpreter*. This is time-consuming and problematical in many ways. The cost of a profes-

sional interpreter is prohibitive, so one may be forced to rely on relatives, neighbors, or friends. This makes it possible to convey and receive simple factual messages, but even here there are hazards. The interpreter may be forced to carry an unwelcome burden. Young children who interpret for their parents are thrust into a role in which the parent is dependent on the child. Children may be kept out of school to help the parent deal with many different institutions in the English-speaking world. Relatives and friends may have a partisan view of the client's situation and may convey their own perception of the problem rather than the client's. The interviewer can never be sure of the accuracy of the translation. Sometimes the interpreter becomes, in an odd way, a member of a group of clients, rather than a conveyor of information.

2. *Employment of indigenous paraprofessionals who are given limited responsibility.* This is a frustrating situation for competent workers who want more responsibility as their confidence in their own usefulness increases. To be employed on "soft money" (government or foundation funds that have an uncertain future) and to have no clear career line will almost inevitably lower the worker's morale.

3. *Employment of indigenous paraprofessionals who are given extensive in-service training and adequate supervision, and carry full responsibility as interviewers.* Even here, lack of a career line is a handicap. The more ambitious and competent of these paraprofessionals might want to complete at least an undergraduate education. They could then become the bilingual and bicultural professionals who are so badly needed.

There are relatively few reports on how well these several alternatives work. Ebihara described a partially successful program for training bilingual paraprofessionals, and sees some utility in this approach.[16] Hardcastle thought that in-service training for nonprofessionals may diminish the very qualities that make their status as indigenous workers valuable.[17]

A more wide-ranging collection of articles can be found

in Padilla's report of a 1977 conference of psychiatrists who work with Spanish-speaking patients.[18] St. Elizabeth's Hospital decided not to establish a separate Spanish-speaking unit, for the Spanish-speaking therapists believed that such segregation would impede acculturation and therefore work to the patients' disadvantage. In this large institution there were enough bilingual professionals so that it was possible to call on them as needed in the many different units. Another report indicated a willingness to use an interpreter, though working through an interpreter takes twice as long. Here it was noted that Anglo therapists were excessively aware of their own inadequacy, and that Spanish-speaking patients did not *always* dislike Anglos. The lack of a common language still leaves the nonverbal language of pictures, signs, gestures, and touching.

Perhaps "feeling for" and "feeling with" the client are expressed as much by the non-verbal language as by words. This is what makes it possible to establish a relationship even when direct communication in words is close to impossible. I suspect that the possession of a common language sometimes leads interviewers to assume erroneously that they and the client share a common view of the world, and this can lead to misunderstanding the client's true concerns.

Notes

1. Webster's *Third New International Dictionary,* Unabridged (Springfield, Mass.: G.C. Merriam Co., Publishers, 1976), p. 1879.

2. National Association of Social Workers, *Encyclopedia of Social Work,* 16th ed. (Washington, D.C.: National Association of Social Workers, 1977).

3. Jacob Bronowski, *The Ascent of Man* (Boston/Toronto: Little Brown, 1973), p. 92.

4. James A. Goodman, ed., *Dynamics of Racism in Social Work Practice* (Washington, D.C.: National Association of Social Workers, 1973).

5. See, for examples, the detective stories by Tony Hillerman, which bring out the tribal differences among the Navajos as well as individual differences within the tribe. One of these novels is *Listening Woman* (New York: Harper and Row, 1978).

6. See, for example, Kim's study of Asian-Americans in Chicago, which details differences in problem-solving strategies characteristic of Chinese, Japanese, Koreans and Filipinos. Bok-Lim C. Kim, *The Asian Americans: Changing Patterns, Changing Needs* (Montclair, N.J.: Association of Korean Scholars in North America, 1978).

7. George Banks, "The Effects of Race on the One-To-One Helping Interview," *Social Service Review,* Vol. 45 (June 1971), pp. 137-46; Franklin T. Barrett and Felice Perlmutter, "Black Clients and White Workers: A Report from the Field," *Child Welfare,* Vol. 51 (January 1972), pp. 19-24; and Alfred Kadushin, "The Racial Factor in the Interview," *Social Work,* Vol. 17 (May 1972), pp. 93-98.

8. Kadushin, *op. cit.*

9. Emelicia Mizio, "White Worker-Minority Client," *Social Work*, Vol. 17 (May 1972), pp. 82-86.

10. Sandra Silverstein, "White Ghetto Worker," *Child Welfare*, Vol. 55 (April 1976), pp. 257-68.

11. Andra Cross, "The Black Experience: Its Importance in the Treatment of Black Clients," *Child Welfare*, Vol. 53 (March 1974), pp. 158-66.

12. Celia Medina and Maria R. Reyes "Dilemmas of Chicana Counselors," *Social Work*, Vol. 21 (November 1976), pp. 515-17.

13. Luciano A. Santa Cruz and Dean H. Hepworth, "News and Views," *Social Casework*, Vol. 56 (January 1975), pp. 52-57.

14. Shirley Cooper, "A Look At the Effect of Racism on Clinical Work," *Social Casework*, Vol. 54 (February 1973), pp. 76-84.

15. Carolyn L. Attneuve, "Therapy in Tribal Settings and Urban Network Intervention," *Family Processes*, Vol. 8 (1979) pp. 192-210; and Ronald G. Lewis and Man Keung Ho, "Social Work with Native Americans," *Social Work*, Vol. 20 (September 1975), pp. 379-82.

16. Henry Ebihara, "A Training Program for Bilingual Paraprofessionals," *Social Casework*, Vol. 60 (May 1979), pp. 274-81.

17. David A. Hardcastle, "The Indigenous Non-Professional in the Social Service Bureaucracy: A Critical Examination," *Social Work*, Vol. 16 (April 1971), pp. 56-63.

18. Eligio R. Padilla and Amade M. Padilla, eds., *Transcultural Psychiatry: An Hispanic Perspective* (Los Angeles: Spanish Speaking Mental Health Research Center, 1977).

Chapter
9

The Use of Time

There are several aspects of the use of time in the interview that call for separate consideration. How long should an interview last? How frequently should interviews take place? Should interviews be at regular or irregular intervals? Over what period of time should interviews occur? It seems obvious that the answers to these questions should be based on the needs of the particular client. It is nevertheless true that agencies and workers sometimes establish such rigid patterns of behavior that consideration of the individual client is scarcely taken into account.

Length and Frequency of Interviews in Relation to the Situation

Regularly scheduled interviews that fit the conventional time patterns of hours and weeks are convenient for administrative purposes, but may not be effective in serving certain clients. One-hour weekly interviews over a period of several months are an appropriate pattern for some counseling agencies whose clientele usually do not present emergencies and who are residents of the area. Agencies geared to emergencies (such as medical settings and Travelers Aid) are of necessity far more flexible in their arrangement of time. In such settings the worker is under constant pressure to make decisions about which things must be done immediately and which things can be postponed.[1] The runaway child or the escaped mental patient who arrives at Travelers Aid may need several hours of continuous contact, or intermittent contact over a period of two or three days. Similarly, emergencies related to hospital admission or discharge may require intermittent contact with patients and their families during a relatively short span of time. Some psychiatric agencies serving a wide geographic area have found ways of making productive use of monthly contacts with the family, involving a concentrated period of counseling over a space of a day or two.

It is increasingly apparent that conventional nine to five office hours do not fit the needs of all clients. Evening and weekend office hours must be available if adequate service is to be given. In institutions where families tend to visit over the weekends rather than during weekdays, it is important for the interviewer to be available to see them. All of this requires careful administrative planning so that services can be given with due consideration for the staff as well as for the clients. The interviewer contributes to the administrative planning by an awareness of clients' needs.

A significant interview can be as short as five minutes or as long as several hours. The contacts can be as frequent as several times in one day or as widely spaced as once a month or once in three months. The total span of contact may be twenty-four hours or several years. Emergency situations and crisis intervention[2] usually call for an intensive period of contact over a short span of time. Less pressing situations in which a specific problem is to be worked on usually call for regular contact weekly, biweekly, or monthly over a period of a few weeks or months. Long-term situations (such as the family with a chronically ill patient or the child in long-term foster care) may call for periods of intensive contact and other periods of more widely spaced interviews.

When the worker is attached to institutions such as hospitals, child care institutions, or nursing homes, the frequent and casual contact with the client on the ward, in the hallways, or in the recreation rooms may be of tremendous value as sustaining measures affirming the client's individuality and expressing a continued interest in the client as a person. Such contacts also make clear the interviewer's availability and make it possible for the client to ask for a more extended conversation when it is needed. However brief the interview, it is important that the client feel a sense of interviewer's full attention.

Planning Time Limits

We have spoken here of the frequency and total span of time of interviews in terms of the acuteness or chronicity of the problem and the nature of the immediate task. Another element to consider in planning interviews also has been touched on elsewhere: the degree of fatigue or other impediments that may be apparent in the client. To the extent that it is feasible, it also is good to give consideration to the optimum concentration period for the interviewer. Some interviewers can give their attention most fully and spontaneously to the client in relatively short interviews of thirty to forty-five minutes. Other interviewers find that they need a sort of warm-up period before their best work is done in the discussion with the client, and they may be able to go on for a longer period of time. As a rule of thumb, somewhere between forty-five minutes and an hour and a quarter seems to be a tolerable limit for both client and worker.[3]

In general, clients should have a fairly clear idea of how much time is available for a particular interview, how frequently the worker will be able to see them, and over what length of time these interviews will take place. Knowledge of approximate time limits removes some of the ambiguity from the situation, and clients do not then have to worry that they are imposing on the interviewer or taking more time than they should. It also has been noted that a knowledge of time limits (both of the interview itself and of the total number of interviews) makes for a different use of time both by the client and the interviewer.[4] A study of family counseling offered convincing evidence that in certain types of problems there is a better outcome when a brief period of time is planned for in the beginning — eight or ten interviews within a period of three months — than when no terminal point is set in the initial contact.[5] It seems possible that the knowledge of time limits motivates both the client and the interviewer to a higher degree of specificity in working on the problem situation. In the planning of time, of course, the cultural differences noted in the last two chapters should be considered.

It is not suggested that time limits be so rigidly adhered to that worker and client are always conscious of the stopwatch ticking in the background. The task to be accomplished in a particular interview may be so obvious to both parties concerned that it is not necessary to mention the amount of time that will be involved. It would be artificial for the interviewer to say: "This interview will take ten minutes because the amount of information that you are asking for will take me that long to give you." On the other hand, in other situations the client's use of time may itself become part of the subject matter of the interview. When clients are consistently silent, or when they find it impossible to start talking about things that matter to them until late in the interview, or when they save all the important comments until the end of the interview, it may be desirable for the worker to point this out and ask what is happening.

Interviewers often have noticed that some of the most important things a client says are at the beginning or at the end of the interview. It is not unusual for a client to start to leave the interviewing room and then turn back to say casually: "Oh, by the way, I really had a fight with my wife last night," Or, "I decided to quit my job and have made a new application." The general rule in other than emergency situations (and, of course, it is never possible for interviewers to be absolutely certain that they have accurately gauged the degree of emergency) is to recognize the client's parting statement but not prolong the interview. The interviewer might say: "This sounds like something we should talk about when you come in next Thursday." The purpose of this kind of activity on the part of the worker is to help the client focus on the important topics early enough in an interview so that these can be dealt with adequately.

Some clients find it difficult to end an interview. Without quite knowing what they are doing, they will embark on a long and complicated discussion just before the end of the time allowed. This seems to arise from their need to control a situation in which they imagine that they are at the mercy of the interviewer. This goes back to the feeling about dependency commented on earlier. There is no magical technique by which interviewers can terminate such an encounter; their ability to end the interview depends on their conviction that the ending is indicated and that they can initiate ending without damaging the client. Occasionally interviewers may need to be quite forceful. They may have to say, "We have no more time today and will have to continue this when you come back," and then rise from the chair, open the door, and suggest that the client leave. They may have to say that someone else is waiting to see them or (if that is not the case) that they have other obligations they must meet.

Beginning interviewers often feel that this kind of behavior will hurt clients or will make them feel that the interviewer does not care about them. Experience will show that clients actually are not injured and may even be helped to focus on the things that are important. Interviewers may have to try this out several times before they gain the confidence to take such action easily and without conflict.

There is a considerable difference in the degree of intensity in the interchange between interviewer and client during a time-limited interview of an hour or less, and a prolonged contact that may last for several hours. For example, if a worker is taking a six-year-old girl to visit a prospective foster home, the worker may spend a whole day with her. Part of the interchange between the child and the worker involves a concentrated and goal-directed discussion. There are other parts of the day when conversation is very casual or when very little talk occurs. Neither the child nor the worker would be able to maintain intense concentration on the problem at hand for so long a period, and this should not be expected.

Notes

1. The classic reference on brief contacts is by Fern Lowry, "Case-Work Principles for Guiding the Worker in Contacts of Short Duration," *Social Service Review*, Vol. 22 (June 1948), pp. 234-39. Also see Ann W. Shyne, "What Research Tells Us about Short-Term Cases in Family Agencies," *Social Casework*, Vol. 37 (May 1957), pp. 223-31. This includes a summary of several studies and a good short bibliography.

2. Howard Parad, ed., *Crisis Intervention* (New York: Family Service Association of America, 1968); Larry Smith, "A Review of Crisis Intervention Theory," *Social Casework*, Vol. 59 (July 1978), pp. 396-405; and Martin Strickler and Margaret Bonnefil, "Crisis Intervention and Social Casework: Similarities and Differences in Problem Solving," *Clinical Social Work Journal*, Vol. 2 (Spring 1974), pp. 36-44.

3. See Robert E. Simmone, "The Brief Interview as a Means of Increasing Service," *Social Casework*, Vol. 48 (July 1967), pp. 429-32, who argues for the thirty-minute interview. He feels that it is nearly as effective as the fifty-minute interview, and it obviously saves time and money.

4. Functional writers (Jessie Taft, Virginia P. Robinson, and the many contributors to *The Journal of Social Work Process*) have made notable contributions in respect to the use of time. More recent books presenting the Functional orientation are: Ruth E. Smalley, *Theory for Social Work Practice* (New York: Columbia University Press, 1967); and Alan Keith-Lucas, *Giving and Taking Help* (Chapel Hill, N.C.: University of North Carolina Press, 1972).

5. Empirical research on the use of time is reported by William J. Reid and Ann W. Shyne, *Brief and Extended Casework* (New York: Columbia University Press, 1969).

Chapter
10

Physical Setting
of the Interview

The physical setting in which the interview takes place has some influence on the content of the interview but perhaps less than is sometimes imagined. The conventional office setting (with the interview taking place in a private room and not in a room with many desks, many interviewers, and many clients) provides a degree of comfort and privacy that is usually considered desirable. For some clients, however, the office setting may be intimidating. Furthermore, there are many situations in which an office interview is impractical. The client who is housebound because of illness must be seen at home; the hospitalized patient must frequently be seen on the ward with other patients in the same room; the setting of groupwork practice may preclude the possibility of a private office interview. Some clients should be seen at home because they have responsibilities there and cannot arrange for someone else to carry those responsibilities while they visit the office. It should be noted, however, that there are areas in large cities unsafe for interviewers to visit a client's home.

The exigencies of a situation may require that interviews be held in crowded clinic waiting rooms, bus stations, or airline terminals. An interview conducted in the presence of others obviously will be different in tone from an interview conducted in private, but even in crowded places the interviewer can create some sense of privacy by giving undiluted attention to the client. Oddly enough, it is easier to create this feeling of privacy in a very crowded place than in a situation where there are only two or three observers. A small number of observers tend to become participants in the interview, sometimes with the active cooperation of the client.

Interviews conducted in the client's home have certain characteristics that differ markedly from interviews conducted in the office. In one sense, clients have less control over the interview in their own homes, and in another sense have more control over it. They have less control over the exact time of the interviewer's arrival and departure than they have over their own arrival at the office and departure from the interview. (They can, of course, take such extreme measures as being absent from home at the time the interviewer has scheduled a visit.)

In many ways, however, clients can affect the atmosphere in their own homes in such a way as to make a productive interview possible or impossible. Usually it is possible for them to insure a degree of privacy, or to make sure that there is no privacy. This is evident in the way that they handle children's activity, telephone calls, or the visits of neighbors. They can regulate the noise level—particularly the TV set. The housewife can indicate her avoidance of the interview situation by continuing to run the vacuum cleaner or continuing with other household tasks that preclude talk. Some people are so accustomed to living with a high noise level that they are not aware that this might interfere with a serious discussion. Interviewers may have to ask (sometimes more than once) that the television or the radio be turned down so that they can hear what the client is saying. If there is too much interruption from children or visitors, they may have to terminate the interview and ask the client about arranging a more suitable time. Common sense suggests that interviews should not be scheduled at a time when the mother is preparing the children's lunch or at a time when the children are expected home from school and will require special attention.

Sometimes a home interview is planned in order to talk with all members of the family. Home visits, like other interviews, are most likely to be useful if there is a mutual understanding of the general purpose of the visit, the time that will be involved, and the persons who will be talking together.[1]

One other thing to consider in a home visit is the extent to which clients feel that they have the obligations of a host on a social occasion. It is not unusual for clients to offer the interviewer refreshments such as coffee or tea. Usually this is a simple human courtesy, and a simple acceptance is indicated. On some occasions it may be extremely important psychologically for clients to offer something such as this to the interviewer, even when it costs more than they can afford. Sometimes, however, the social interchange involved in tea and cake becomes a means of avoiding the work in which the client and interviewer are engaged. When interviewers become aware of this, they may be able to refuse politely ("No thanks, not today. I have just come from lunch."). If simple measures like this do not work and the avoidance is repeated, the interviewer may have to discuss it openly by some such comment as: "I have noticed that when we stop for coffee it always takes us a long time to get back to the job we have to do. Let's not have it today."

A comment was made earlier about interruption from visitors during a home visit. Interviewers here need to be alert to the client's willingness to introduce them. Some clients may avoid an introduction completely, and it may be apparent that they would prefer the visitor not know that the interviewer is from a social agency. This is the client's business and the interviewer needs to follow the client's lead in this.

Note

1. Martin A. Bloom, "Usefulness of the Home Visit for Diagnosis and Treatment," *Social Casework,* Vol. 54 (February 1973), pp. 67-75.

Chapter
11
Persons Involved
in the Interview

Human beings do not live in a vacuum; they have connections with family, friends, job, school, and many other institutions. The interviewer who seeks to help an individual also must take account of and sometimes become involved with the persons and institutions that are of importance to clients in their current situation.[1] The discussion so far, however, has not taken into account the decisions that are made about who is to be interviewed. In casework practice, it is sometimes assumed that the person who comes to the agency is labeled the "client," and that interviews with other members of the family or household are incidental and perhaps peripheral to the service received by this client.[2] A number of other patterns are possible, singly or in combination:

1. Individual interviews with two or more members of a family.
2. Joint interviews with two members of the family.
3. Interviews with the entire family or household group.

In any of these patterns it is possible to have one or two interviewers (occasionally more than two) involved. Family members may be seen individually by different workers, and it also is possible for two workers to meet with the clients in a multiple interview.[3] After interviews with other family members, it occasionally becomes evident that a person other than the "labeled" client must be considered the primary focus of attention.

Interviewing Other Family Members

The nature of the presenting problem or the immediate task at hand is sometimes a clear indicator of the desirability of engaging additional members of the family either individually or jointly in interviews. Consider, for example, such situations as the following: the family seeking institutional care for a mentally retarded child; the family asking for nursing home care for an aged member; the family with an adolescent child who has been in trouble with the law and placed in detention; the family preparing to receive a member who is being discharged from a medical or psychiatric institution; the family expecting to receive someone who is to be discharged from prison; the family wanting to adopt a child; or the family wanting to give up a child for adoption. All these examples deal with changes in the family composition, accompanying changes in the family role, and in some instances, changes in the family's use of its material resources. It is not only the person who is being added to or subtracted from the family group who needs to be considered in situation like these.

Whether one sees the additional members individually or jointly is still debatable. When joint planning is needed and joint decisions must be reached, common sense suggests that the persons involved should be seen together. There is less likelihood of subsequent misunderstanding if all persons concerned are present at the same time in the interview situation.

There are times, however, when multiple interviews are fruitless. Sometimes family members are so antagonistic toward each other that they are unable to consider the issues jointly;

sometimes one member of the family is so cowed by the others that this member is unable to speak freely when they all meet; and occasionally one member of the family feels the problem so deeply and intensely as to be unable to express personal feelings in the presence of the group. Such a person might well prefer an opportunity to talk privately with the worker.

Multiple Interviews

Multiple interviews involve interaction among the persons being interviewed, as well as interaction between them individually and the interviewer. As such, the demands placed on interviewers have a dimension that differs from the demands placed on them in an interview with one person. In the individual interview, workers are listening to what clients tell them about their interaction with other people in real life, and are also observing the way in which the clients are responding to them. In multiple interviewing, by contrast, workers are listening to what the clients are saying to each other as well as to what they are saying to them. They are observing the interaction of these people in their real life relationships. The field of observation is much larger and it is harder to keep track of all the things taking place.

If interviewers are accustomed to talking to just one person at a time, they often find themselves — in the multiple interview — conducting what is in effect a series of individual interviews in the presence of additional people. Although this may be appropriate at certain points, the major benefits of multiple interviewing are derived from the clients talking to each other rather than carrying on individual interchanges with the interviewer. The interviewer's activity then becomes one of encouraging this direct communication between members of the family, commenting on areas of agreement and understanding or disagreement and misunderstanding, commenting on patterns of communication, raising questions about the goals that the clients have in mind (either in terms of decisions that must be made, planning that has to be undertaken, or changes in communication patterns that are desired), suggesting ways of reaching the desired goals, and summarizing what has been achieved.

The multiple interview also may make special demands on interviewers' emotional resources, as well as on their attention. Individuals in the group may make a bid for attention or may attempt to enlist support in partisan warfare. Interviewers would be inhuman if they were impervious to such efforts. In order to make an appropriate response they must first face their own feelings—their resentment at the client's efforts to get them to take sides, their preference for one client versus another, or their sympathy for a particular point of view or way of presenting that point of view. If interviewers are aware of their own feelings, they will be less likely to make damaging use of them and can be more helpful in pointing out to the family what it is they are doing. When the pattern becomes apparent, the interviewer might comment on it in terms such as the following: "It sounds to me as if you are trying to get me to take sides against your wife in this matter and I am not sure where that will get you in working on this problem." Or, "I have the uneasy feeling that you all look at me as an all-powerful judge who can make a perfect decision."

Group Counseling

Social workers in agencies that historically have focused their helping efforts on the individual and the family are increasingly being called on to work with groups of clients who are brought together because they have some problem or concern in common. Group counseling cannot, strictly speaking, be called interviewing, and a lengthy discussion of its techniques does not belong in this volume. This form of helping clients in groups has some things in common with multiple interviewing with the family: interviewers direct their attention to the interaction among the members of the group and try to facilitate this as a means of enabling the group members to help each other. The family, however, is bound together over a long period of time, and even when its members are physically separated, it has an important influence on the individual. The family is inherently a hierarchical structure. In the formed group, the association is usually temporary and for a particular purpose. Its members are peers, and they are not held together by ties of blood and long-standing connections.

It is a common practice for groups of clients to be brought together for several discussion sessions at the point of orientation to an institution or in preparation for discharge from an institution. Patients who share the same living quarters in a hospital often are brought together for the discussion of the problems related to their life in the institution or of the problems that brought them to the institution and with which they will still have to deal. In family agencies, public assistance agencies, and other open settings, discussion groups of various kinds have been found to be helpful — some have focused on the tangible realities of getting along on a public assistance budget, and some have focused on such interpersonal problems as marital conflict or parent-child relationships.

Selection of group members, formation of the group, establishment of group goals, patterns of interaction among group members, decisions about time limits, the worker's role in the group, and appropriate activity in the group — all these constitute a subject area beyond the scope of this book. Skill in individual and family interviewing is by no means irrelevant, but additional knowledge and technical competence must be acquired if the interviewer is to become an effective group counselor.[4]

Notes

1. Carel B. Germain, "The Ecological Perspective in Casework Practice," *Social Casework*, Vol. 54 (June 1973), pp. 323-30.

2. Work with persons outside the household will be considered in Chapter 13.

3. The choice of interviewing pattern depends in part on the interviewer's skills and theoretical orientation. Some theorists believe that all psychological and interpersonal problems are essentially problems of the total family, and that therefore the entire family regularly must be included in conferences. The concept of family treatment is currently enjoying considerable popularity. The literature since 1960 is so voluminous that even a selected bibliography becomes unwieldy. A few references follow: Nathan W. Ackerman, Frances L. Beatman, and Sanford N. Sherman, eds., *Expanding Theory and Practice in Family Therapy* (New York: Family Service Association of America, 1967); Richard Bendler, John Grinder, and Virginia Satir, *Changing with Families* (Palo Alto, Calif.: Science and Behavior Books, 1976); Scott Briar, "The Family as an Organization: An Approach to Family Diagnosis and Treatment," *Social Service Review*, Vol. 38 (September 1964), pp. 247-55; Donald F. Krill, "Family Interviewing as an Intake Diagnostic Method," *Social Work*, Vol. 13 (April 1968), pp. 56-63; Arthur L. Leader, "Current and Future Issues in Family Therapy," *Social Service Review*, Vol. 43 (March 1969), pp. 1-11; Dwaine R. Lindberg and Anne W. Wosmek, "The Use of Family Sessions in Foster Home Care," *Social Casework*, Vol. 44 (March 1963), pp. 137-41; Frances H. Scherz, "Multiple-Client Interviewing: Treatment Implications," *Social Casework*, Vol. 43 (March 1962), pp. 120-25; and Sanford N. Sherman, "Aspects of Family Interviewing Critical for Staff Training and Education," *Social Service Review*, Vol. 40 (September 1966), pp. 302-308.

4. The following contain examples of the use of groups in connection with casework: Hans S. Falck, "The Use of Groups in the Practice of Social Work," *Social Casework*, Vol. 44 (February 1963), pp. 63-67; Norman Fenton and Kermit T. Wiltse, eds., *Group Methods in the Public Welfare Program* (Palo Alto, Calif.: Pacific Books, 1963); and Albertina Mably, "Group Application Interviews in a Family Agency," *Social Casework*, Vol. 47 (March 1966), pp. 158-64. Also see the following analyses and reviews of the literature: Mary E. Burns and Paul H. Glasser, "Similarities and Differences in Casework and Group Work Practice," *Social Service Review*, Vol. 37 (December 1963), pp. 416-28; Louise A. Frey and Ralph L. Kolodny, "Illusions and Realities in Current Social Work with Groups," *Social Work*, Vol. 9 (April 1964), pp. 80-89; and Barbara Rostov, "Group Work in a Psychiatric Hospital: A Critical Review of the Literature," *Social Work*, Vol. 10 (January 1965), pp. 23-31.

Chapter 12

The Influence of Theory on the Conduct of the Interview

Much of the discussion of individual interviewing so far has been focused on initial interviews. Mention has been made of the "disciplined expression of interest" as a method of helping the client talk about relevant matters. But how do interviewers know what is relevant? How do they know what they should pay attention to? Although common sense dictates some of the answers, much also depends on the interviewers' theoretical orientation: their view of human behavior and of the helping process. At the risk of oversimplification, some of the gross differences between a few major current theories will be summarized.[1]

Dynamic psychology has been profoundly influential in American casework for the last half-century. Within this general orientation, which owes much to Freud[2] and those who came after him, there are several schools of thought that present certain identifiable differences. "Psychosocial," "functional," and "problem-solving" theorists all perceive past experience and current environment as having an important influence on present behavior, but there are some differences in emphasis.

The psychosocial theorist places emphasis on developmental history and early experiences as determinants of present feelings and attitudes, and a major objective of counseling is to help clients understand the nature of their feelings and behavior, and, in some instances, to understand their origin. The functional school places emphasis on the here-and-now of the way clients are making use of agency resources and relating to the worker. Beginning and ending, union and separation, the wish to engage oneself and the resistance to such engagement are seen as fundamental life experiences finding their prototype in the client's connection with the agency. Hence the present relationship with the worker and the attitudes toward what the agency has to offer, as well as toward the limitations implied both in time and services, are a major focus of the interview. The experience of this relationship and an understanding of it is expected to enhance the capacity of clients to manage their lives.

In the problem-solving frame of reference, the casework situation is seen as a special instance of the problem-solving process that is part of everyday life. Clients' perceptions of their problems, the nature and strength of their desire to do something about them, the resources that they have within themselves and that are available in their environment, the ways in which they have tried to deal with the problems in the past, the degree of success or failure that they have experienced in these previous efforts, and the way in which they can make use of help are all of import in the initial assessment of the situation. The expectation is that the process of helping clients work on their problems and achieve some degree of success will strengthen their capacity to manage for themselves.

Sociobehaviorist or behavior modification theory is of a somewhat different order. It rests heavily on learning theory as developed by Pavlov and Skinner. The sociobehaviorist's interest is in the client's repertoire of behavior: behavior that needs to be changed, modified, or shaped in a new direction. There is less interest in developmental history and in the client's total personality than in the specific behavioral manifestations that are observable. The expectation is that through the use of such techniques as reinforcement and extinction, the client's behavior will be changed in the desired direction.

These four approaches—psychosocial, functional, problem-solving, and behavior modification—are those presented in the 1977 edition of the *Encyclopedia of Social Work*,[3] but many other theories, approaches, and techniques will be found in the literature of social work, psychology, and psychiatry. Gilbert, Miller, and Specht suggested a taxonomy of the theories most relevant to social work under the major headings of (1) conceptions that locate the problem in the mind, (2) action conceptions, (3) theories locating the problem in an interactional field, and (4) theories that bear on social structure.[4]

Theory affects the interviewers' selection of what to pay attention to in the client's spontaneous productions, and influences their decisions about what to explore further. The interviewers' concept of the range of potentially effective helping measures has a direct bearing on the kinds of things they need to know before they make a selection among the helping measures to be employed.

Though I have found valuable ideas in all the theoretical orientations so briefly presented above, the problem-solving framework appears to have the widest applicability and to lend itself most readily to expansion, development, and modification. Therefore, much of what is presented in this book stems from the problem-solving orientation.

Notes

1. A lucid presentation of several theories, together with a comparative analysis, will be found in Robert W. Roberts and Robert H. Nee, eds., *Theories of Social Casework* (Chicago: University of Chicago Press, 1970). This volume does not include a discussion of the influence of existential philosophy or Carl Rogers' nondirective approach. For these, see, for example, Donald F. Krill, "Existential Psychotherapy and the Problem of Anomie," *Social Work*, Vol. 14 (April 1969), pp. 33-49; and Carl R. Rogers, ed., *The Therapeutic Relationship and Its Impact* (Madison, Wis.: University of Wisconsin Press, 1967). Also see Gerald Corey, *Theory and Practice of Counseling and Psychotherapy* (Monterey, Calif.: Brooks/Cole Publishing Co., 1977). This text covers various current therapies: psychoanalytic, existential-humanistic, client-centered, gestalt therapy, transactional analysis, behavior therapy, rational-emotive therapy, and reality therapy.

2. Helen Harris Perlman, "Freud's Contribution to Social Welfare," *Social Service Review*, Vol. 31 (June 1957), pp. 192-202.

3. National Association of Social Workers, *Encyclopedia of Social Work*, 16th ed. (Washington, D.C.: National Association of Social Workers, 1977).

4. Neil Gilbert, Henry Miller, and Harry Specht, *An Introduction to Social Work Practice* (Englewood Cliffs, N. J.: Prentice-Hall, 1980), pp. 71-79.

Chapter

13

Interviews in Continuing Service

It sounds as though the process of assessing the client's situation was confined to early interviews, and that once this diagnosis had been achieved, a new process called "helping" or "treatment" would begin. Such a separation between two aspects of interviewing is entirely artificial, however. The very act of exploring the problem (trying to define it, reviewing its origins, considering the ways in which it affects various aspects of life, and trying to assess possible courses of action and their consequences) may in itself constitute an important part of the help that the client needs. The problem, or some aspect of it, may then become manageable and the client's own capacity can be brought into play more fully. Furthermore, the act of telling the story to someone who is not overwhelmed by it may serve to put the matter into perspective and make it seem less burdensome. The sense of interest, concern, and confidence conveyed by interviewers both in their words and tone of voice has value for clients and may help them mobilize their own resources.

This initial exploration, in itself an act of helping, has two other purposes. First, as interviewers begin to understand their clients better and to perceive their feelings about their life situation and about the present problem, the interviewers' acceptance of the clients and empathy for them usually become stronger and are more clearly conveyed. Second, a client's account of the situation may give definite indications of the kind of intervention by the interviewer that would be helpful. It may provide tentative answers to the questions: What should be talked about, with whom, and to what purpose?

The techniques used in continuing interviews have much in common with those employed in the initial phase. There is a continuing reexploration of the problem or task presented, or of some aspect of it. There is a continued effort to reach a mutual understanding of the goals being sought, the means that are to be employed in achieving them, and the expectations of the client and the worker. In addition, there is some explicit review of the progress that has been made. As client and worker become better acquainted and have some confidence that they understand each other, laborious and detailed explanations are likely to be less necessary than in the first interview.

Change Objectives

The subject matter of continuing interviews deals with the kind of service that is being given. The client is in contact with the social worker because somebody (either the client or someone in the client's environment) thinks that something should be changed. Agreement on the objective and method forms part of the contract between client and worker. The interviewer is expected to do something to set change in motion.[1] Change efforts may be directed toward the following, singly or in combination:

1. The clients themselves: their fund of knowledge, their patterns of behavior, and their feelings about themselves and others.
2. The clients' material resources or living situation.
3. The persons in the clients' immediate environment:

their fund of knowledge, their patterns of behavior, and their feelings.

4. Social institutions affecting the clients' welfare: persons in such institutions, the structure of the institution, or its functions.

The individual's request for help or someone else's insistence that help be offered does not mean that change efforts are necessarily directed to the client. This point is emphasized because much of the literature on interviewing is related to psychotherapy and is focused on the client's patterns of behavior, feelings, and self-awareness.

An important part of social work practice, however, deals with other kinds of change. The initial and continuing task of diagnosis or assessment is to reach an understanding with the client of what ought to be changed, what can be changed, and what immediate steps can be taken to effect change that will at least ameliorate a troublesome situation. Social workers are appropriately concerned with changing public attitudes, improving administrative arrangements, and enacting legislation that will have long-term benefits for persons in need. But the client who is ill today cannot wait for a new hospital to be built. Immediate help involves the use of existing resources, whether these are adequate or inadequate.

Provision of Goods and Services

The provision of goods and services (such things as money, housing, institutional care, foster care, medical care, psychiatric care, summer camp, vocational counseling, legal aid, or homemaker service) may be accomplished directly through the agency's own resources or through other resources. Making arrangements with other agencies may involve no more than giving the client information, though frequently it requires a formal referral, and occasionally the interviewer acts as mediator or advocate.[2]

Referral to Resources

To make an appropriate referral to another resource requires knowledge both of the clients and their needs, and of the agency and other community resources and the services they can offer. Occasionally clients make it clear that all they need is information. A mother may say that she knows her children should be vaccinated, and then will ask the worker to give her the name of the clinic most convenient to her residence.

Often, however, the situation is not so clear cut, and interviewers will need to do a good deal more than simply write down an address and telephone number for the client. Workers need to know exactly what services are given by the agency and the conditions under which those services are offered. Do the clients want any of these services? Are they able to meet the conditions that are set? Do they know how to get to the agency? What are the office hours? Is it necessary to make an appointment ahead of time? Must clients make the appointment themselves or is it possible for the worker to do so? Should a referral slip be given to clients to take to the new agency? Should a referral letter also be sent? Does the agency have a waiting list? How long might it be before clients can be seen? Have clients heard about this agency before or used it before, and do they have some impression of what might be involved in going there?

These are some of the questions that come to mind as client and interviewer discuss the possibilities of a referral. Clients are more likely to be able to use the services of another agency if they have an accurate idea of what to expect and how to go about making an application. Inaccurate or incomplete information (resulting, for example, in sending the client to a clinic on a Friday when new applications are taken only on Thursdays) constitutes an impediment to the use of the service. Some clients may need to rehearse for future action. What shall they wear when they go to the employment office? What are they expected to tell the vocational counselor? In more extreme instances, clients may almost be paralyzed with fright about making an application elsewhere and may need the physical presence of the interviewer or of a volunteer attached to the agency in order to mobilize themselves in using another resource.[3]

In the course of making a referral, especially if the situation is complex, the interviewer will have considerable contact (by telephone, in person, or by letter) with the other agency. The quality of the relationship between workers in two agencies has more to do with interagency cooperation than all the administrative memoranda that are written. In making a referral, one of the major items to remember is that a particular service cannot be "ordered": it is not like writing a prescription for a druggist to fill.

The receiving agency may be able to give the interviewer a general idea about the probable eligibility of the client, but the referring worker cannot guarantee to the client that a specific service will be given in a specific way. This decision is up to the agency to which the client applies.

Working with the Client in Providing Services

The provision of goods and services, either through one's own agency or through referral to another resource, may involve considerable direct work with clients and their feelings: feelings about asking for and receiving help, feelings about the relationship with the worker or the agency, or feelings about the implications of the particular service involved. The sense of powerlessness and dependency which clients may struggle against, submit to, or even revel in has been alluded to earlier. When such feelings appear, they may be in part a product of a client's past experiences, in part a response to the worker's behavior and attitude, and in part a reaction to the implications of the particular service being offered. To the extent that the service offered is vital to the clients' existence or has implications for a marked change in their existence, and to the extent that the agency has actual power to give or withhold such service, the clients' emotional responses will be a factor to consider.

Two examples of this are the provision of income to cover basic necessities, and the services involving placement. Foster care, adoption, and all types of institutional placements imply a temporary or permanent separation from a familiar way of life and a new beginning in an unfamiliar setting. Decisions about separations are not made lightly. The family who seeks nursing home care for an aged, ill relative, the parents who ask for permanent placement of a mentally retarded child, the mother who asks that her child be placed out for adoption — such people usually have already experienced some conflict or are experiencing it at the time of the request. If the conflict is not adequately resolved, the placement will be sabotaged either by the person who is placed or by those who have arranged the placement. This means that the interviewer has to be particularly sensitive to signs of ambivalence, guilt, or hostility, and must make it possible for the clients and their families to talk about these feelings.

There are many ways in which the topics could be opened up, depending on the situation. Questions might be asked such as: "Let's talk about the pros and cons of this plan." "Have you been separated from your child before? How did it feel then?" "Have you been away from home before? How was it then?" "Do you have some ideas about what this is going to be like?" It is important to explore these topics, since separation is often equated with death, desertion, or abandonment, and therefore arouses strong and sometimes irrational and ungovernable emotions. Interviewers cannot assume that such emotions always exist. Their job is to make it possible to talk about them if they do exist.

A distinction should be drawn between a bland, glassy, totally unemotional surface attitude that suggests an attempt to prevent strong feelings from erupting, and the thoughtful rational response that suggests alternatives have been considered and the implications of placement have been faced. The interviewer's objective is to avoid skimming over an issue when it is in fact important, and at the same time avoid creating an issue when none exists. When a service that arouses so much feeling is offered by one's own agency, it is clearly the responsibility of the interviewer to work with the feeling. When the client is being referred elsewhere for such service, the interviewer's responsibility is similar, but might not be so extensive.

Failure of a Referral

There are times when a referral, even though it has been thoroughly discussed with the client and carefully carried out, simply does not work. Bureaucratic structure, administrative regulations, application forms, and special eligibility requirements can all become so complicated that they form an obstacle to the client's use of service. The worker has some responsibility to try to straighten out such difficulties, either by communicating directly with the other agency, or by seeking interagency communication between supervisors or administrators. Vituperation and accusations of incompetence are not calculated to insure good service to this client or to others.

Sometimes a carefully made referral fails because clients, having presented themselves at the cooperating agency, behave in such a way that the application is refused. They may ask for a service that the agency is not equipped to give, or act as though their request were trivial and they did not really want any service, or behave with such angry belligerence that an interview becomes impossible. They may fail to meet the conditions under which help is given by refusing to give information, by missing interviews, or by consistently coming at the wrong time. The failure of the referral then becomes the topic of the referring interviewer's discussions with the client. This starts as an exploration of a new facet of the problem: What happened? What does the client want? What might be the next steps?

Sometimes it becomes apparent that preparation for the referral was inadequate. The clients' knowledge of the available services and the necessary procedures may have been inadequate, or their feelings about the service for which they were applying may have been insufficiently discussed. Sometimes rather pervasive patterns of behavior emerge, and the interviewer will then try to help the client make connections: "Was this the same sort of thing that happened when you first came in here?" "Sometimes it almost seems as if you are trying to prevent people from helping you."

The interviewer's own feelings about the referral also may affect the outcome. When interviewers are deeply concerned about the client, they may fear that no one else will work strenuously enough on the client's behalf. Will any one else understand the client so well? Will anyone else care so much? They even may feel reluctant to share their helping functions with another agency. If they are unaware of such feelings and therefore have no control over them, this inevitably will be expressed in some way to the client. There are no technical interviewing tricks that will take care of this situation. The only protection is self-understanding on the part of interviewers, which in turn leads to changes in the way they handle their feelings.

Helping the Client To Change

This extended discussion of interviewing in connection with referrals is an indication of the ways in which, while providing or arranging for changes in the client's material resources, changes also may be effected within the client. The interviewer engages in a constellation of verbal activities, and the emphasis on one or another element is related to the nature of the problem, the objectives that are sought, and the attributes of the persons concerned.[4]

It is helpful for interviewers to have some notion of the various dimensions by which an interview can be described, since this enables them to analyze their own activities and locate the points at which some alteration in their behavior may benefit the client. A conceptual framework improves the chances of repeating one's successes and reducing the number of one's failures.

The following major dimensions are suggested as a guide to an analysis of an interview:

1. The nature of the change objectives (as outlined at the beginning of this section).
2. The subjects discussed: external objective facts, internal subjective feelings (which also are facts), the self, the other, the relationship with others, the relationship with the worker, the past, the present, and the future.
3. The level of verbal activity of client and worker: the extent to which the client initiates and continues the discussion, and the extent to which the worker is active in this regard.[5]
4. The degree of mutuality: the extent to which client and worker are joined in a common purpose, or the extent to which they are divided or working at cross-purposes.

Interviewers are responsible for what they say and do. It is the client, not the interviewer, who makes choices about a course of action—granted that circumstances sometimes sharply limit the range of choice. The worker seeks to provide an opportunity for clients to make full use of their capacity to make responsible choices. The worker's activities of listening, observing, and helping clients explore the situation and (when relevant) their feelings about it are characteristic of continuing service as well as beginning interviews.

Hope for a solution to difficulties is expressed in many ways: through open recognition of competence clients have shown in the past or present; through breaking up the problem into smaller parts so that it is not so overwhelming; or through helping clients locate some aspect of the problem that they can solve and thus gain some sense of mastery. The interviewer expresses an expectation—always within realistic limits—of the client's accomplishment.[6] In an atmosphere of confidence and trust, workers can point out inconsistencies in what clients say and do, and can help them make connections between feelings, actions, and consequences. They can help clients prepare for certain experiences and support their moves toward taking action. There are times when interviewers can respond directly to evidence of a client's feelings about them and initiate a discussion of the relationship. They can then review what has been achieved.

Working with Persons in the Environment on Behalf of the Client

Let us now consider helping efforts that are directed toward persons in the client's environment. This was touched on earlier in the discussion of multiple interviewing and family interviewing (see Chapter 11). There are many instances in which family interviewing is impractical or undesirable. There may be family members who refuse to become engaged or who are themselves so disturbed or antagonistic that their presence would be disruptive in an interview. There are times when family members may be unwilling to ask for help themselves, since they see no necessity for this, but are sufficiently concerned about the identified client to be willing to try to understand that person better and to modify some of their own behavior. This is a situation in which a misunderstanding about the implied contract easily can arise. Family members may not see themselves as persons to be helped, whereas the worker may see the matter quite differently. A change in focus from "How can I help you to understand Mary?" to "How can I help you to understand yourself?" must sooner or later be put into words so that family members can make a deliberate choice about the degree of their commitment.

There are numerous occasions when the interviewer is called on—with the client's knowledge—to give information about the client or the client's situation to family members, other persons in the immediate environment, or to personnel in such institutions as the school or medical care facilities. Such contacts may be so brief and their content so self-evident that they are scarcely thought of as interviews, much less interviews that have as their purpose changing the persons in the client's environment.

Yet we operate on the assumption that knowledge changes feelings, attitudes, and behavior, sometimes in trivial ways and sometimes with far-reaching effect. When we tell a foster parent or cottage parent about a child's eating habits or sleeping routines, it is with the expectation that the foster parent either will adjust to the child's own routine or will have some tolerance for the child's difficulty in adapting to changed routines. When we tell a member of the household about the limitations imposed by a medical problem on a client's activity, it is with the expectation that some adjustments can be made in relation to the client's needs. When we tell someone about the kind of behavior that can be expected in the light of the client's past experiences or in the light of a particular medical or psychiatric condition, it is with the expectation that this information will change the attitudes or behavior of the person concerned.

Persons receiving such information usually have a reaction to it: they ask questions, they volunteer information of their own, or they indicate the effect that this information has on themselves. Nobody is merely an appendage to the person who may be the center of interest for the worker. Thus interviewers will find that even though they have initiated the contact for the specific purpose of giving information, and see themselves as the chief actor in the interview, the basic principles of interviewing still apply. If the interview is to result in a mutual view of the situation, the interviewer must listen as well as talk.

Notes

1. The concept of the worker as a "change agent" carries the unfortunate connotation of manipulation, but this is not the intent. For a formulation of the steps involved in accomplishing change, see Ronald Lippitt, Jeanne Watson, and Bruce Westley, *The Dynamics of Planned Change* (New York: Harcourt Brace, 1958).

2. Joseph J. Parnicky, David L. Anderson, Charles M.L.S. Nakoa, and William T. Thomas, "A Study of the Effectiveness of Referrals,"*Social Casework*, Vol. 42 (December 1961), pp. 494-501.

3. The concept of "preparation and accompaniment," which applies to many situations other than referrals, is described by Ethel J. Panter in her article, "Ego-Building Procedures that Foster Social Functioning," *Social Casework*, Vol. 47 (March 1966), pp. 139-45.

4. There have been many efforts to classify various forms of helping activity. Florence Hollis reviews these in *Casework: A Psychosocial Therapy* (New York: Random House, 1964). Hollis and her associates have reported a number of empirical studies of interviewing in counseling situations. The most comprehensive single reference is Hollis's pamphlet, *A Typology of Casework Treatment* (New York: Family Service Association of America, 1968). Another kind of description of interview content will be found in Margaret Schubert, *Field Instruction in Social Casework* (Chicago: University of Chicago School of Social Service Administration, 1963). The development of this schedule stems from Lilian Ripple's work, *Motivation, Capacity, and Opportunity* (Chicago: University of Chicago School of Social Service Administration, 1964). Also see Shulman's report of research on clients' assessment of social workers' behavior: Lawrence Shulman, "A Study of Practice Skills," *Social Work*, Vol. 23 (July 1978), pp. 274-80.

5. A particularly good analysis of the levels of interviewer activity will be found in Jacob E. Finesinger, "Psychiatric Interviewing," *American Journal of Psychiatry*, Vol. 105 (September 1948), pp. 187-96.

6. Genevieve B. Oxley, "The Caseworker's Expectations and Client Motivation," *Social Casework*, Vol. 47 (July 1966), pp. 432-37.

Chapter
14

The Use of Telephone Calls and Letters

The Telephone As an Interviewing Medium

The telephone is an important interviewing medium, sometimes as a supplement to face-to-face interviews, sometimes as the major (or even sole) means of communication.[1]

In agencies dealing with crisis intervention and suicide prevention, telephone contacts are essential, and usually are available to clients on a 24-hour basis. Working with such clients requires all the ordinary skills of interviewing, but the need for skill is intensified because one depends solely on one's voice.

A telephone conversation is disembodied; the participants cannot see each other and can pick up only the verbal clues, not the nonverbal communication. Participants already well-

acquainted with each other may scarcely be aware of this disembodied quality, for they imagine what the other person looks
like. This mental picture may be inaccurate, and this means that
workers will need to express themselves more fully in words and
guard against their own tendency to make assumptions about
what clients mean based on what they say.

The telephone interview between two persons who have
never seen each other presents somewhat different problems. Each
participant develops a mental image of the other person, and this
image is inevitably incorrect. Interviewers can convey themselves
only through words and tone of voice. There is no way that they
can pick up the client's nonverbal communication—the indications of disturbance or lack of understanding sometimes shown so
clearly in face-to-face communication even when the client is silent.
Therefore, in the telephone interview, one's attention is focused
even more sharply on the rate of speech, interruptions, silences,
sighs, and tone of voice. Even in the face-to-face interview it is
difficult to tolerate and evaluate silences, and it is doubly so in
the telephone interview.

In crisis intervention agencies, the telephone calls usually
are unscheduled. There are other situations, however, in which
scheduled telephone interviews are regularly planned. For example,
in agencies for the physically handicapped, both interviewer and
client may be handicapped, and thus home calls as well as office
visits are impractical. Here arrangements can be made for a regular
telephone call at a specified time—perhaps for 30 minutes once a
week, perhaps for other lengths of time at other intervals.

Another sort of planned telephone interview can be
arranged for continued contact when the client is geographically
removed and does not have access to other sources of help. Such
interviews probably should be for a specified length of time on a
given day and hour. This lends some structure to the situation and
can stimulate both client and worker to focus on the client's
problem, talk over plans for action, express and respond to feelings,
and review progress—in short, all the things that the worker seeks
to do in a face-to-face interview.

Even when planned telephone interviews are not a major
medium, there usually are a number of occasions when calls are
initiated by either the client or the interviewer. When these are
limited to such routine matters as confirmation of an appointment,
they present no great difficulty. However, calls often are initiated
by clients out of a sense of emergency, and such calls may come as

an interruption to the interviewer, or at a time when it is impossible to talk freely. The interviewer needs to give recognition to the client's feeling of urgency or emergency, even if it is impossible to continue the conversation at that moment and an arrangement has to be made to return the call at a specific time. When the client has a request that can be dealt with in a short period of time, the unplanned emergency telephone call presents no great problem. When the conversation is less well-focused or when there is some recognition that it will be prolonged, interviewers may have to set some time limit. They might have to say something such as: "I have another appointment in twenty minutes but until then we can talk." Or, "There are some other things I need to do this afternoon, but I have half an hour now."

Frequent and aimless telephone calls may represent a degree of impulsivity or an insatiable demand on the part of the client that may become a part of the interviewer's understanding of the situation, and thus might have to be dealt with in interviews. Some impulsive clients who fear their own loss of control in dealing with (for example) explosive family conflicts are encouraged to telephone when this fear comes upon them, which forestalls them from acting on impulse.

The interviewer often is called on to initiate telephone contact with relatives or others who are concerned about the client's welfare and with whom there has been no previous contact. Under such circumstances, interviewers should identify themselves clearly and indicate the reason for the call. It is only common courtesy to ask immediately if the call is at a convenient time and if the person they are calling is free to talk. It is not unusual for such a telephone call, particularly if it is long distance, to arouse anxiety in the recipient, who might be thinking: "What disaster has occurred now?" "I wonder what they want me to do?" "I have all I can bear at the present time and I don't want anything more." "Whatever it is they want, I am not going to do it." With the recognition of such possibilities, the interviewer is in a better position to listen to the person at the other end of the line, to offer reassurance as indicated, and to establish some sort of communication.

The telephone is so commonly used in communicating with colleagues and with other agencies that one scarcely thinks of such contacts as requiring any special skill. The common courtesy suggested above, of course, applies here as well. Clarity of focus will make the phone call more productive. And, as always, the interviewer has to listen as well as talk. There is one special hazard in telephone communications with other agencies: one tends to be less guarded in a phone call than in a letter, and particular attention must be paid lest one violate confidentiality.

Few of us know what our voice really sounds like on the phone. Some people answer the telephone with a welcoming voice, some with a tone that seems to repel the caller; some sound cheerful (whether they are or not), and some sound depressed (whether they are or not). In crisis intervention, it is desirable to convey a degree of neutrality of mood. In all situations it is help- ful to express, in tone of voice, a note of readiness to hear and respond. Interviewers should think of this when they evaluate their telephone interviews.

Letters

Letters, whether they are addressed to a client, a relative, or another agency, require the same thoughtfulness that goes into an interview in person or by telephone. Reports to agencies, while they may be something of a chore, are perhaps the simplest of written communications. Clarity of purpose, relevant focus, and brevity are essential; and courtesy, either in making a request or responding to a request, dictates that one should be neither demanding nor condescending.

A prompt and thoughtful response to an agency's re- quest can do much to increase cooperation among agencies in the interest of maximum service to the client. Acknowledgment of a referral, either by letter or telephone, is supposed to be a regular part of agency practice, but occurs much less frequently in reality than it should.

During a number of years as a caseworker, only once did I receive a report from an agency to whom I had referred a client. This changed my whole attitude toward the agency, which I had previously regarded as rather stuffy, and led me to feel freer to discuss potential referrals with them. In all this one must of course observe the requirements of confidentiality outlined in Chapter 6.

Letters to clients often are much more difficult to write. In letters, interviewers are even more separated from the client than in telephone interviews. The distrustful or suspicious client can twist words, worry over them, or distort their intent. Some- how interviewers have to avoid too much distance or too much intimacy. After a broken appointment with such a person, a telephone call is preferable to a letter, but if a letter is the only means of communication, perhaps something like this will do: "I missed you last week, and I'm holding your usual time for you at 10 o'clock Friday." Even this can be interpreted as the writer's need for the client, or as an excessive demand being made. The interviewer's only consolation here is that nobody has devised a perfect letter to fit such a situation.

There are other kinds of written communications that serve to sustain contact during vacations or other brief absences. Such uses are suggested in Chapter 15. Picture postcards with even just a brief message give a clear indication that the client has not been forgotten.

At times, geographical distance and lack of convenient and inexpensive telephone connections dictate that letters must be used as a means of helping. One way for the interviewer to deal with this is to arrange in advance to set aside an hour each week to read the client's letter and respond to it. Similar plans can be worked out in areas where, for example, an intensive two-day family treatment session in a psychiatric setting occurs every two or three months, and interim communication is deemed desirable.

After all this discussion, it seems apparent that letters and telephone calls deserve careful consideration by the interviewer, both in providing direct help to the client and in working with others who are concerned about the client's welfare.

Note

1. There is very little social work literature on the use of the telephone and letters. A comprehensive summary of the use of the telephone from the psychiatrist's point of view is offered by Warren B. Miller, "The Telephone in Outpatient Psychotherapy," in *Psychiatric Treatment: Crisis/Clinic/Consultation*, ed. Peter Rosenbaum and John E. Beebe III (New York: McGraw-Hill, 1975), pp. 423-32. Also see Margaret E. Adams, "First Aid to Parents of Retarded Children," *Social Casework*, Vol. 48 (March 1967), pp. 148-53; the vivid description of the telephone interview (in a suicide prevention service) in Monica Dickens' novel, *The End of the Line* (Garden City, N.Y.: Doubleday, 1970); and Ervin B. Zentner, "The Use of Letters to Sustain the Casework Process," *Social Casework*, Vol. 48 (March 1967), pp. 135-40.

Chapter
15
Ending

The end of the contact between client and worker occurs for a variety of reasons: the planned termination comes about by mutual agreement when previously specified goals have been achieved; other terminations sometimes are initiated by the client, sometimes by the worker.[1]

The Mutually Planned Termination

In some cases, ending is such a simple and inevitable process that its components are scarcely noticed. Consider, for example, the reasonably self-directing family that asks for help in obtaining nursing home care for an aged member. The interviewer explores with them the nature of the problem, the reactions of the various family members, the implications of placement, the re-sources the family and others can bring to bear in this situation, and the possible consequences of the various alternatives. A need for nursing home care is established and a suitable placement is found; the placement is satisfactorily arranged. While the persons concerned are not under the illusion that all their life problems have been solved, they have received the services from the agency that they were expecting. They thank the worker and proceed to move ahead with their own lives.

In this simple illustration, the end has been visualized in the beginning and is mutually perceived by the persons involved. The goal is clear, specific, and realistically limited. The family's capacity for making decisions has not been impeded or impaired. The relationship between the family and the interviewer is based in reality. The interviewer and the family assess the problem in the same way and see the same solution as appropriate. There has been no attempt to change the original contract or make a shift in goals.

However, endings are not always so easy. Complex and relatively recalcitrant problem situations, profound dependency needs on the part of the client, an intense relationship with the interviewer with overtones of transference manifestations, and a prolonged period of contact—all tend to make the termination process more difficult. When the prospect of ending is discussed, clients may try to make the situation tolerable for themselves through various means. They suddenly may cancel appointments or be very late for an appointment, as if they were saying that the interviewer was not going to end with them, but that they were going to end with the interviewer. Or emergencies may arise: clients may have an accident or illness or engage in anti-social behavior so that the interviewer is forced to delay termination. Sometimes they will bring up completely new problems or start giving the worker information about aspects of their life history that never had been touched on before. They may find various ways of expressing a sense of helplessness and worthlessness, or they may become angry with the worker over some triviality in an entirely uncharacteristic way.

To the extent that ending represents to clients rejection, abandonment, desertion, or even death, they will (without being aware of what they are doing) make some attempt to control such an intolerable and fearful situation. Interviewers' perceptions of these possibilities will make them less impatient with a client's seemingly irrational behavior at such times. Sometimes all that is needed in a situation of this kind is the interviewer's continued steadiness and calmness. Clients' unusual behavior may subside and they may give indications of movement toward termination. Clients may be able to accept the worker's affirmation of their competence as they review together the gains that have been made, the problems that remain, and their ability to deal with those problems at some level.

If the unusual behavior is extreme or protracted, it may be necessary for interviewers to help clients identify it and understand some of the reasons that it is occuring. This sometimes can be done in a few words without making an issue of the matter. For example: "Does this really seem like the end of the world?" Or, "It sounds as if it were rather hard for you to let go right now." Or, "You know, I really am not going to forget all about you." Occasionally, depending on the situation, the interviewer can try to help clients make a connection between their reactions to this experience and to other experiences in the past. For example: "I remember your telling me how you felt the time that your mother put you in a foster home. Are you feeling a little like that now?" Sometimes the interviewer may have to move beyond this and quite directly bring up the problem that the client is experiencing in relation to termination. For example: "You usually don't miss interviews and you usually don't act so mad at me. I am beginning to think that you have some pretty strong feelings about ending these interviews and I think it would be a good idea if we tried to understand what's going on."

The Interviewer's Responsibility in Working Toward Ending: The Importance of Self-Awareness

Examples have been given of termination processes that are inherently simple and inherently complex. Interviewers cannot, in any absolute sense, control the termination process any more than they can control the problem itself or the client's behavior. There are, nevertheless, some things that they can do which will help reduce the difficulties of ending. Ending has its roots in the beginning—the understanding that is reached between worker and client about the task they hope to accomplish and the circumstances under which the contact will be terminated. If interviewers consciously or unconsciously expect to create new personalities for

their clients in the hope that they will be able to cope successfully with all conceivable life situations, or if they expect to
sustain their clients through all the problems they meet, no ending
will be in sight. If, on the other hand, interviewers help clients
establish more limited goals, then there is some realistic possibility
that the task can be completed. When, in the course of a long
contact, new goals begin to emerge or a change in direction seems
desirable, interviewers can help clarify such changes. This process
of clarification, in turn, will help promote the possibility of the
client making an active and responsible choice.

The interviewers' personal feelings about a client are
sometimes an impediment to termination. When interviewers
are unconsciously gratified by the client's dependence on them,
they may show their reluctance to end the contact in various
ways: by failing to recognize or affirm the progress that has been
made; by failing to recognize the clients' signals that they are
ready to end; by discovering or anticipating new problems that
require help; or by fearing that clients will see termination as
abandonment. These are some of the signs which indicate that
workers need to reflect on their own behavior and become aware
of their feelings in order to manage them for the client's benefit.

After a prolonged series of interviews, how does one
introduce the subject of termination? If the original "contract"
included an approximate statement of the length of time that
would be required, interviewers might remind the client of this
and suggest that they review together what has been accomplished
so far and what they want to do in the time remaining. If the time
limits have not been suggested earlier, but there are signs of the
client's growing competence and independence, workers might
bring up the subject with some such comment as: "It seems to
me you are about ready to go it alone." Or, "I think you have
accomplished quite a bit in dealing with this problem. Let's
take a look at where we started and where we are now, and how
much more time we need."

As one moves toward termination, the accent should be
on affirmation of what clients have done, an expression of confidence in their future competence, and helping them affirm this
independently. The words "case closed" do not, of course, mean
that the client can never return to the agency. The possibility of
future help should be made clear. It is appropriate for the interviewer to express a continued interest in and positive feelings
toward the client.

Termination Initiated by the Client

The client sometimes initiates the termination by failing to return after a first interview or by cutting short the contact before a satisfactory outcome has been achieved. These events are difficult to evaluate, and it is even more difficult for interviewers to decide whether they should offer encouragement to return through a letter or telephone call. The client surely has a right to refuse service, and even when service is forced on the "unwilling" client (described in Chapter 2) such a person effectively can refuse to become engaged in making use of the service.

In cases of child abuse or in other situations where there is some clear danger involved, continued efforts to reach out are necessary. But when such factors are not present, the worker is in a quandary. Was the purpose of the contact insufficiently understood in the beginning? Has the interviewer failed to explain what would be involved in working together on the problem presented? Did the interviewer move too quickly in touching on sensitive points so that the client has withdrawn in self-protection? Have things progressed so slowly that the client feels further work is useless? Or has something entirely extraneous to the helping situation caused the client to terminate?

I can offer no hard and fast advice on this situation. In general, if interviewers sense that clients have been feeling worthless and unwanted, a follow-up probably is indicated, either by telephone or by letter, provided that clients have not kept their visits a secret from their family or close associates. A telephone call is preferable to a letter, since on the telephone interviewers can convey their concern through their tone of voice and can be responsive to the client's words and tone. A letter is inevitably a less personal message and easily can be interpreted in ways that the interviewer has not intended.

First, of course, interviewers have to be sure that they are trying to meet the client's needs rather than their own; they have to avoid pushing for an emotional closeness that is more than the client wants; and they must phrase their communication in such a way that they leave the door open for the client to return, but also to stay away if the client so chooses. The substance of the interviewers' message should be that they recognize the client's decision but are still available in case of need.

Other client-initiated terminations are less problematic: the client is moving to another city or to a location that precludes a trip to the office; or increased family responsibilities or changed hours of employment make regular interviews impractical. In these cases, interviewers sometimes can help the situation by referral to another agency, or by the sustaining contact of letters or phone calls. When time permits, one or two final interviews can be helpful in clarifying with clients the extent of their achievement to date, what they can do independently, and how they can obtain further help when needed.

Termination Initiated by the Worker

Interviewers are not permanent fixtures in an agency. They change jobs within the agency, they go to other agencies, they move to other cities for family reasons or for other employment. Sometimes they suffer illness that creates a prolonged absence. They take vacations, which might be termed a break in service, but which have some of the characteristics of termination. Students are placed in an agency for a specific period of time, and terminations are present from the very beginning.

Whenever time limits are known in advance, I believe that it is desirable to let the client know as early as possible what these time limits are. This advice is irrelevant when in the first interview it seems clear that the client can be helped to reach the desired goal within the time available. But there are some types of counselling in which a series of interviews over a period of many months is anticipated. In some situations the client is hospitalized in a psychiatric facility for prolonged periods, during which the social worker carries a sustaining role. Also, children in institutions or in foster care need help over a long period of time. In these instances there is an obligation to let the client know what to expect of the worker.

It sometimes happens that even if an interviewer informs the client in February that the interviewer will be on vacation for three weeks in May, this is "forgotten." I am not suggesting that interviewers keep hammering this information into the client's head, but rather that it is wise to be sensitive to the client's awareness or lack of awareness, and bring up the matter again a few weeks before going on vacation. For some clients (adults whose emotional stability is marginal, institutionalized persons, or children in placement) postcards sent while the interviewer is away are a useful sustaining measure.

A change of jobs within the agency or departure from the agency by a worker requires a careful assessment of the desirability of transferring a client to another worker. Sometimes the client will use the option of terminating contact rather than seeing another interviewer. When the client is transferred to another worker in the same agency, some effort usually is made to assure continuity of service. It is desirable to introduce the client to the new interviewer and sometimes it is helpful to have a joint conference. The main thing that interviewers need to realize, however, is that the contact with the new worker is in a sense a new beginning. Their willingness to give up the client and their recognition that this new beginning must take place are more important than any procedures one might establish. The interviewer who cannot give up a client will somehow manage to deprecate the competence of the new interviewer or otherwise sabotage the continuation of service. Rivalry between staff members or a lack of mutual respect will reduce the opportunity for the client to make full use of the agency's services. Such feelings have to be dealt with by each worker independently of the client.

When termination occurs because of the worker's departure from the agency and not because of the client's readiness to terminate, one can expect that feelings about the relationship will find expression. If there is a strong element of dependency on the part of the client, feelings of abandonment and resentment about this desertion will appear. Interviewers may feel guilty about leaving a client in the lurch. They may find themselves clinging to the relationship and trying to make up to the client for their defection. Once again, self-awareness will be an important factor in enabling them to keep their mind on the client's needs rather than their own. During this terminal phase, discussion of the content of the relationship and its meaning to the client is sometimes appropriate, but the interviewer needs to avoid attributing a meaning to this that the client does not feel.

If the relationship between client and worker has been prolonged and intense, the worker's absence because of serious long-term illness will almost inevitably cause the client a great deal of concern. Another interviewer, trying to help the client work on the problem as originally defined, can anticipate some sort of reaction—rational or irrational—from the client. It is natural for the client to want news of the first worker's health: "How is Mr. Robinson feeling? When will he be back? Was the operation very serious?" But sometimes there are exaggerated fears, a pretense of indifference, an all-too-quick appreciation of the new interviewer, a withdrawal from the new worker's helping efforts, or open animosity. Such responses can be maddening or gratifying, and require the new interviewer's utmost skill. This is, once again, a beginning for client and worker, but a beginning that is tinged with the emotions felt toward the previous worker.

One other kind of ending, which does not fit neatly into any of the above categories, occurs in cases in which termination is administratively determined. Examples of these are the adolescent with a one-year probationary period, or the child under care who reaches adult status. The client who is "unwilling" to begin with and is still "unwilling" at the end is glad to terminate (and termination can be something of a relief to the frustrated interviewer). But at times such a person gradually has become "willing," recognizes a need for further help, and wants to use it. When the agency is not permitted to offer further help, referral elsewhere is indicated if at all feasible. This involves both the ending process discussed above, and the referral process described in Chapter 13.

Much of the preceding has focused on the problematic aspects of breaks in service and terminations. Not all endings are traumatic. Interviewers should not make mountains out of molehills!

Note

1. Most texts on casework contain some discussion of termination. Much of the periodical literature focuses on the termination process in psychiatric settings. A few references are suggested: Martha Grossman and Harriett Guignon, "Group Study of the Transfer of Cases," *Social Casework*, Vol. 33 (June 1952), pp. 241-46; Sidney Z. Moss and Meriam S. Moss, "When a Caseworker Leaves an Agency: The Impact on Worker and Client," *Social Casework*, Vol. 48 (July 1967), pp. 433-37; Evelyn F. Fox, Marian A. Nelson, and William M. Bolman, "The Termination Process: A Neglected Dimension in Social Work," *Social Work*, Vol. 14 (October 1969), pp. 53-63; and Hilliard L. Levinson, "Termination of Psychotherapy: Some Salient Issues," *Social Casework*, Vol. 58 (October 1977), pp. 480-89. An earlier publication concerned with a rather specialized group of clients is Regina Flesch, *Treatment Consideration in the Reassignment of Clients* (New York: Family Service Association of America, 1947).

Chapter
16

The Client-Worker Relationship: Recapitulation

Frequent reference has been made to the worker-client relationship and the way it is manifested in the interview.[1] A brief summary follows.

A good working relationship is characterized by a sense of trust on the part of the client—confidence that the worker is trying to understand, is willing to listen, is able to help, and values the client as a person. Such a working relationship is not necessarily smooth, bland, or polite. In fact, if clients are truly free to talk, they may express negative feelings about their situation, and on occasion about the worker or the agency. A purposeful relationship of this kind, in which feelings are not markedly distorted and are appropriately expressed, is referred to as "rapport."

Because ways of relating to people are learned over a long period of time and become fairly well-established at an early age, one always brings past experience into a current relationship. Sometimes the client's behavior toward the worker and feelings about the worker appear to be entirely unconnected with the reality of the present situation. Freudian theory explains this on the basis of "transference"—feelings toward significant persons in one's infancy are inappropriately transferred to the worker, so that the client may be acting toward the worker as if this person were a parent. Such feelings are unconscious and not under the client's voluntary control. An awareness of this possibility will help the interviewer tolerate some of the client's seemingly irrational behavior.

The social work interview is not designed to encourage the development of a transference; although transference phenomena may sometimes require discussion, such discussion is seldom an essential part of the helping process. The spacing of interviews, the face-to-face position of client and interviewer, and the subjects discussed are planned to encourage a focus on current realities rather than on fantasies about early parental relationships.

Sometimes clients are close to an awareness of their irrational behavior, and it then may be helpful to acknowledge this. When a client says: "You remind me so much of my mother," the worker could respond by saying: "And do you expect me to behave the same way?" This may be sufficient to point out the reality of the present situation. Sometimes, when it appears that transference feelings are interfering with a client's use of the interview, the worker might find it useful to make some such comment as: "There is something odd about all this. I almost have the feeling that you are expecting me to behave the way your father did in this situation." There are disagreements among theorists about the validity of these interpretations or about their importance, but it seems reasonable to suppose that persons who are in a position of dependency will bring to this experience emotions that they have felt in an earlier dependent position.

Another aspect of the relationship mentioned often in the preceding pages is the worker's feelings toward the client. Some writers label all these feelings as "counter-transference." The label is most appropriately applied when the interviewer's feelings are not related to the reality of the present situation, but are distorted by past experience that is inappropriately brought into the present relationship. Interviewers always have feelings about the client—positive or negative, superficial or profound, intense or mild, realistic or irrational, conscious or unconscious. They cannot control or channel such feelings unless they are aware of them.

As noted in the last chapter on "Ending," the termination of the worker-client contact is a point at which any existing problematic aspects of the relationship are likely to surface. Some observers have found that workers tend to minimize the importance of relationships in brief contacts, and overemphasize it in long-term cases.[2] This easily could happen because of the sheer quantity of the worker's investment in long-term contacts. This overvaluation is one of the signals that workers should assess and manage their own responses to the client.

Notes

1. The various writers previously mentioned (Garrett, Hamilton, Hollis, Perlman, Robinson, Rogers, Smalley, and Towle) have much to say about the nature of the relationship. The most extensive book on the subject, written from the standpoint of social work practice, is Helen Harris Perlman, *Relationship: The Heart of Helping* (Chicago: University of Chicago Press, 1979). Also see some of the earlier publications: Felix P. Biestek, "An Analysis of the Casework Relationship," *Social Casework,* Vol. 35 (February 1954), pp. 57-61; Annette Garrett, "The Worker-Client Relationship," in *Ego-Psychology and Dynamic Casework,* ed. Howard J. Parad (New York: Family Service Association of America, 1958); and Richard Sterba, Benjamin H. Lyndon, and Anna Katz, *Transference in Casework* (New York: Family Service Association of America, 1948). Two articles, written from the psychoanalytic point of view, offer helpful clarification on the concept of transference: S.V. Silverberg, "The Concept of Transference," *Psychoanalytic Quarterly,* Vol. 17 (July 1948), pp. 303-21; and Maurice Levine, "Principles of Psychiatric Treatment," in *Dynamic Psychiatry,* ed Franz Alexander and Helen Ross (Chicago: University of Chicago Press, 1952).

2. Carlton E. Munson and Pallassana Balgopal, "The Worker-Client Relationship: Relevant Role Theory," *Journal of Sociology and Social Welfare,* Vol. 5 (May 1978), pp. 404-17.

Chapter

17

The Rules Reexamined

The basic rules are simple, but, as this presentation attests, they are not always easy to follow. For interviewers to give their full attention requires that they be intellectually and emotionally free to attend. Attention is always selective, since no one can observe and respond to every aspect of a life experience. Indeed, to attend to everything equally would make the experience unmanageable. If the basis of the interviewers' selectivity (theoretical framework, biases, feelings, and predelictions) is conscious, it is more nearly subject to their control, and the range of their awareness of the client can be extended. This in turn improves their chances of avoiding unwarranted assumptions about what the client thinks, feels, or does, and they will be quicker to recognize the points at which they need to ask questions in order to clarify meaning. The objective is to arrive at that mutual view of the situation and of the goals that will contribute to carrying out a joint purpose with the client.

Much emphasis has been placed on the discipline required of the interviewer. How can this be reconciled with the human spontaneity that is so essential a component in any vital interchange? It has been suggested that the discipline is slowly achieved; it is acquired in the course of reflection and analysis that take place outside the interview, and eventually it can be exercised within the interview. Interviewers change and can use this changed self genuinely in talking with the client. Oddly enough, the more confident they become of their self-awareness and self-discipline, the freer they will be in responding to the client. They can admit ignorance or puzzlement, recognize mistakes, and express feelings more easily.

The equipment that interviewers start with is their interest and concern. Although these qualities cannot be learned in an intellectual sense, they can be enhanced and augmented by increased knowledge. There are times when interviewers' positive feelings for the client may lead them into trouble, but trouble of this kind is less damaging than the aridity of indifference or of routinized responses to client requests or comments.

It should be evident by now that there is no one way of conducting an interview. Some guidelines have been offered and some specific suggestions have been made about ways of dealing with certain situations. The scope of these suggestions is necessarily limited. As interviewers gain specialized experience (with certain age groups, for example, or particular constellations of problems, or people with certain physical, emotional, cultural, or social attributes) they will find their own means of responding to clients in ways that will help them make maximum use of the interview.

Bibliography

Ackerman, Nathan W.; Frances L. Beatman; and Sanford N. Sherman, eds. *Expanding Theory and Practice in Family Therapy.* New York: Family Service Association of America, 1967.

Adams, Margaret E. "First Aid to Parents of Retarded Children." *Social Casework* 48 (March 1967): 148-53.

Alger, Ian, and Peter Hogan. "Enduring Effects of Videotape Playback Experience on Family and Marital Relationships." *American Journal of Orthopsychiatry* 39 (January 1969): 86-98.

Aronson, H., and Betty Overall. "Treatment Expectations of Patients in Two Social Classes." *Social Work* 11 (January 1966): 35-41.

Attneuve, Carolyn L. "Therapy in Tribal Settings and Urban Network Intervention." *Family Processes* 8 (1979): 192-210.

Banks, George. "The Effects of Race on the One-to-One Helping Interview." *Social Service Review* 45 (June 1971): 137-46.

Barrett, Franklin T., and Felice Perlmutter. "Black Clients and White Workers: A Report from the Field." *Child Welfare* 51 (January 1972): 19-24.

Bartlett, Harriett M. *The Common Base of Social Work Practice.* New York: National Association of Social Workers, 1970.

Bendler, Richard; John Grinder; and Virginia Satir. *Changing with Families.* Palo Alto, Calif.: Science and Behavior Books, 1976.

Bernstein, Saul. "Self-Determination: King or Citizen in the Realm of Values?" *Social Work* 5 (January 1960): 3-8.

Biestek, Felix P. "An Analysis of the Casework Relationship." *Social Casework* 35 (February 1954): 57-61.

_____. "The Principle of Client Self-Determination." *Social Casework* 32 (November 1951): 369-75.

Bloom, M.A. "Usefulness of the Home Visit for Diagnosis and Treatment." *Social Casework* 54 (February 1973): 67-75.

Briar, Scott. "The Family as an Organization: An Approach to Family Diagnosis and Treatment." *Social Service Review* 38 (September 1964): 247-55.

Bronowski, Jacob. *The Ascent of Man.* Boston: Little Brown, 1973.

Burns, Mary E., and Paul H. Glasser. "Similarities and Differences in Casework and Group Work Practice." *Social Service Review* 37 (December 1963): 416-28.

Chevigny, Hector, and Sydell Braverman. *The Adjustment of the Blind.* New Haven, Conn: Yale University Press, 1950.

Compton, Beulah R., and Burt Galaway. *Social Work Processes.* Homewood, Ill.: The Dorsey Press, 1975.

Cooper, Shirley. "A Look at the Effect of Racism on Clinical Work." *Social Casework* 54 (February 1973): 76-84.

Corey, Gerald. *Theory and Practice of Counseling and Psychotherapy.* Monterey, Calif.: Brooks/Cole, 1977.

Cormican, John D. "Linguistic Subcultures and Social Work Practice." *Social Casework* 57 (November 1976): 589-92.

_____. "Linguistic Issues in Interviewing." *Social Casework* 59 (March 1978): 145-51.

Cross, Andra. "The Black Experience: Its Importance in the Treatment of Black Clients." *Child Welfare* 53 (March 1974): 158-66.

Davis, Allison. *Social Class Influences Upon Learning.* Cambridge, Mass.: Harvard University Press, 1950.

Dick, Kenneth, and Lydia J. Strnad. "The Multi-Problem Family and Problems of Service." *Social Casework* 39 (June 1958): 349-55.

Dickens, Monica. *The End of the Line.* Garden City, N. Y.: Doubleday, 1970.

Ebihara, Henry. "A Training Program for Bilingual Paraprofessionals." *Social Casework* 60 (May 1979): 274-81.

Egan, Gerard. *The Skilled Helper.* Monterey, Calif.: Brooks/Cole, 1975.

Evans, David R.; Margaret T. Hearn; Max R. Uhlmann; and Allen E. Ivey, *Essential Interviewing.* Monterey, Calif.: Brooks/Cole, 1979.

Falck, Hans S. "The Use of Groups in the Practice of Social Work." *Social Casework* 44 (February 1963): 63-67.

Fenton, Norman, and Kermit T. Wiltse, eds. *Group Methods in the Public Welfare Program.* Palo Alto, Calif: Pacific Books, 1963.

Finesinger, Jacob E. "Psychiatric Interviewing." *American Journal of Psychiatry* 105 (September 1948): 187-96.

Flesch, Regina. *Treatment Considerations in the Reassignment of Clients.* New York: Family Service Association of America, 1947.

Fox, Evelyn F.; Marian A. Nelson; and William M. Bolman. "The Termination Process: A Neglected Dimension in Social Work." *Social Work* 14 (October 1969): 53-63.

Frey, Louise A., and Ralph L. Kolodny. "Illusions and Realities in Current Social Work with Groups." *Social Work* 9 (April 1964): 80-89.

Garrett, Annette. *Interviewing: Its Principles and Methods.* 2nd ed., rev. New York: Family Service Association of America, 1972.

———. "The Worker-Client Relationship." In *Ego Psychology and Dynamic Casework,* edited by Howard J. Parad. New York: Family Service Association of America, 1958.

Germain, Carel B. "Social Study: Past and Future." *Social Casework* 49 (July 1968): 403-409.

———. "The Ecological Perspective in Casework Practice." *Social Casework* 54 (June 1973): 323-30.

Gilbert, Neil; Henry Miller; and Harry Specht. *An Introduction to Social Work Practice.* Englewood Cliffs, N. J.: Prentice-Hall, 1980.

Goodman, James A., ed. *Dynamics of Racism in Social Work Practice.* Washington, D. C.: National Association of Social Workers, 1973.

Gottlieb, Werner, and Joe H. Stanley. "Mutual Goals or Goal-Setting in Casework." *Social Casework* 43 (October 1967): 471-81.

Graff, Harold; Lana Kenig; and Geoffrey Radoff. "Prejudice of Upper-Class Therapists Against Lower-Class Patients." *Psychiatric Quarterly* 45 (1971): 475-89.

Grossman, Martha, and Harriet Guignon. "Group Study of the Transfer of Cases." *Social Casework* 33 (June 1952): 241-46.

Hall, Marny. "Lesbian Families: Cultural and Clinical Issues." *Social Work* 23 (September 1978): 380-85.

Hamilton, Gordon. *Theory and Practice of Social Case Work.* 2nd ed., rev. New York: Columbia University Press, 1951.

Hardcastle, David A. "The Indigenous Non-Professional in the Social Service Bureaucracy: A Critical Examination." *Social Work* 16 (April 1971): 56-63.

Herzog, Elizabeth. "Some Assumptions about the Poor." *Social Service Review* 37 (December 1963): 389-402.

Hillerman, Tony. *Listening Woman.* New York: Harper and Row, 1978.

Hollis, Florence. *Casework: A Psychosocial Therapy.* New York: Random House, 1964.

_____. *A Typology of Casework Treatment.* New York: Family Service Association of America, 1968.

Holmes, Sally; Carol Barnhart; Lucile Cantoni; and Eva Reymer. "Working with the Parent in Child Abuse Cases." *Social Casework* 56 (January 1975): 3-12.

Kadushin, Alfred. *The Social Work Interview.* New York: Columbia University Press, 1972.

_____. "The Racial Factor in the Interview." *Social Work* 17 (May 1972): 93-98.

Kahn, J. P. "Attitudes Toward Recipients of Public Assistance." *Social Casework* 36 (October 1955): 359-65.

Keith-Lucas, Alan. "A Critique of the Principle of Client Self-Determination." *Social Work* 8 (July 1963): 66-71.

_____. *Giving and Taking Help.* Chapel Hill, N. C.: University of North Carolina Press, 1972.

Kim, Bok-Lim C. *The Asian Americans: Changing Patterns, Changing Needs.* Montclair, N. J.: Association of Korean Scholars in North America, 1978.

Kolodny, Ralph L. "Ethnic Cleavages in the United States: An Historical Reminder to Social Workers." *Social Work* 14 (January 1969): 13-23.

Krill, Donald F. "Family Interviewing as an Intake Diagnostic Method." *Social Work* 13 (April 1968): 56-63.

_____. "Existential Psychotherapy and the Problem of Anomie." *Social Work* 14 (April 1969): 33-49.

Lackie, Bruce. "Non-Verbal Communication in Clinical Social Work Practice." *Clinical Social Work Journal* 5 (Spring 1977): 43-52.

Leader, Arthur L. "Current and Future Issues in Family Therapy." *Social Service Review* 43 (March 1969): 1-11.

Levine, Maurice. "Principles of Psychiatric Treatment." In *Dynamic Psychiatry,* edited by Franz Alexander and Helen Ross. Chicago: University of Chicago Press, 1952.

Levinson, Hilliard L. "Termination of Psychotherapy: Some Salient Issues." *Social Casework* 58 (October 1977): 480-89.

Lewis, Ronald G., and Man Keung Ho. "Social Work with Native Americans." *Social Work* 20 (September 1975): 379-82.

Lindberg, Dwaine R., and Anne W. Wosmek. "The Use of Family Sessions in Foster Home Care." *Social Casework* 44 (March 1963): 137-41.

Lindenberg, Ruth Ellen. "Hard to Reach: Client or Casework Agency?" *Social Work* 3 (October 1958): 23-29.

Lippitt, Ronald; Jeanne Watson; and Bruce Westley. *The Dynamics of Planned Change.* New York: Harcourt Brace, 1958.

Lowry, Fern. "Case-Work Principles for Guiding the Worker in Contacts of Short Duration." *Social Service Review* 22 (June 1948): 234-39.

Mably, Albertina. "Group Application Interviews in a Family Agency." *Social Casework* 47 (March 1966): 158-64.

Maluccio, Anthony N., and Wilma D. Marlow. "The Case for the Contract." *Social Work* 19 (January 1974): 28-37.

Mayer, John E., and Noel Timms. *The Client Speaks.* London: Routledge and Kegan Paul, 1970.

Medina, Celia, and Maria R. Reyes, "Dilemmas of Chicana Counselors." *Social Work* 21 (November 1976): 515-17.

Mendes, Helen A. "Countertransference and Counter-Culture Clients." *Social Casework* 58 (March 1977): 159-63.

Mizio, Emelicia. "White Worker-Minority Client." *Social Work* 17 (May 1972): 82-86.

Moss, Sidney Z., and Meriam S. Moss. "When a Caseworker Leaves an Agency: The Impact on Worker and Client." *Social Casework* 48 (July 1967): 433-37.

Miller, Warren B. "The Telephone in Outpatient Therapy." In *Psychiatric Treatment: Crisis/Clinic/Consultation,* edited by Peter Rosenbaum and John E. Beebe. New York: McGraw-Hill, 1975.

Munson, Carlton E., and Pallassana Balgopal. "The Worker/Client Relationship: Relevant Role Theory." *Journal of Sociology and Social Welfare* 5 (May 1978): 404-17.

National Association of Social Workers. *Encyclopedia of Social Work.* 16th ed. Washington, D. C.: National Association of Social Workers, 1977.

Oswald, Ida, and Suzanne Wilson. *This Bag Is not a Toy.* New York: Council on Social Work Education, 1971.

Overton, Alice. "Serving Families Who Don't Want Help." *Social Casework* 34 (July 1953): 305-309.

Oxley, Genevieve B. "The Caseworker's Expectations and Client Motivation." *Social Casework* 47 (July 1966): 432-37.

_____. "Promoting Competence in Involuntary Clients." In *Promoting Competence in Clients,* edited by Anthony N. Maluccio. New York: The Free Press, 1981.

Padilla, Eligio R., and Amado M. Padilla, eds. *Transcultural Psychiatry: An Hispanic Perspective.* Los Angeles: Spanish Speaking Mental Health Research Center, 1977.

Panter, Ethel J. "Ego-Building Procedures that Foster Social Functioning." *Social Casework* 47 (March 1966): 139-45.

Parad, Howard, ed. *Crisis Intervention.* New York: Family Service Association of America, 1965.

Parnicky, Joseph J.; David L. Anderson; Charles M. L. S. Nakoa; and William T. Thomas. "A Study of the Effectiveness of Referrals." *Social Casework* 42 (December 1961): 494-501.

Perlman, Helen Harris. "Freud's Contribution to Social Welfare." *Social Service Review* 31 (June 1957): 192-202.

_____. *Social Casework: A Problem-Solving Process.* Chicago: University of Chicago Press, 1957.

_____. *Persona.* Chicago: University of Chicago Press, 1968.

_____. *Relationship: The Heart of Helping People.* Chicago: University of Chicago Press, 1979.

Rauch, Julia B. "Gender as a Factor in Practice." *Social Work* 23 (September 1978): 388-95.

Reid, William, and Ann Shyne. *Brief and Extended Casework.* New York: Columbia University Press, 1969.

Ripple, Lilian; Ernestina Alexander; and Bernice Polemis. *Motivation, Capacity and Opportunity.* Chicago: University of Chicago School of Social Service Administration, 1964.

Roberts, Robert W., and Robert H. Nee, eds. *Theories of Social Casework.* Chicago: University of Chicago Press, 1970.

Roberts, Robert W., and Helen Northen, eds. *Theories of Social Work with Groups.* New York: Columbia University Press, 1976.

Robinson, Virginia. *A Changing Psychology in Social Case Work.* Chapel Hill, N. C.: University of North Carolina Press, 1930.

Rogers, Carl R., ed. *The Therapeutic Relationship and Its Impact.* Madison, Wis.: University of Wisconsin Press, 1967.

Rostov, Barbara. "Group Work in a Psychiatric Hospital: A Critical Review of the Literature." *Social Work* 10 (January 1965): 23-31.

Santa Cruz, Luciano A., and Dean H. Hepworth. In "News and Views." *Social Casework* 56 (January 1975): 52-57.

Scherz, Frances H. "Multiple-Client Interviewing: Treatment Implications." *Social Casework* 43 (March 1962): 120-25.

Schmidt, Julianna T. "The Use of Purpose in Casework Practice." *Social Work* 14 (January 1969): 77-84.

Schubert, Margaret. *Field Instruction in Social Casework.* Chicago: University of Chicago School of Social Service Administration, 1963.

Schwartz, Mary C. "Importance of the Sex of the Worker and the Client." *Social Work* 19 (March 1974): 177-86.

Selig, A. "The Myth of the Multi-Problem Family." *Journal of Orthopsychiatry* 46 (July 1976): 526-41.

Sherman, Sanford N. "Aspects of Family Interviewing Critical for Staff Training and Education." *Social Service Review* 40 (September 1966): 302-308.

Shulman, Lawrence. "A Study of Practice Skills." *Social Work* 23 (July 1978): 274-80.

Silverberg, S. V. "The Concept of Transference." *Psychoanalytic Quarterly* 17 (July 1948): 303-21.

Silverstein, Sandra. "White Ghetto Worker." *Child Welfare* 55 (April 1976): 257-68.

Simmons, Robert E. "The Brief Interview as a Means of Increasing Service." *Social Casework* 47 (July 1967): 429-32.

Smalley, Ruth. *Theory for Social Work Practice.* New York: Columbia University Press, 1967.

Smith, Larry. "A Review of Crisis Intervention Theory." *Social Casework* 59 (July 1978): 396-405.

Social Casework 52 (May 1971). Special Issue on Chicanos.

————. 55 (February 1974). Special Issue on Social Work and the Puerto Rican Community.

————. 57 (March 1976). Special Issue on Asian and Pacific Islander Americans.

Social Work 17 (May 1972). Special Issue on Ethnicity and Social Work.

————. 21 (November 1976). Special Issue on Women.

Sterba, Richard; Benjamin H. Lyndon; and Anna Katz. *Transference in Casework.* New York: Family Service Association of America, 1948.

Strauss, Emilie T. "The Caseworker Deals with Employment Problems." *Social Casework* 32 (November 1951): 388-92.

Strickler, Martin, and Margaret Bonnefil. "Crisis Intervention and Social Casework: Similarities and Differences in Problem Solving." *Clinical Social Work Journal* 2 (Spring 1974): 36-44.

Studt, Elliot. "An Outline for Study of Social Authority Factors in Casework." *Social Casework* 35 (June 1954): 231-38.

————. "Worker-Client Authority Relationships in Social Work." *Social Work* 4 (January 1959): 18-28.

Sunley, Robert. "New Dimensions in Reaching-Out Casework." *Social Work* 13 (April 1968): 64-74.

Taylor, Robert K. "The Social Control Function in Casework." *Social Casework* 39 (January 1958): 17-21.

Towle, Charlotte. *Common Human Needs.* rev. ed. New York: National Association of Social Workers, 1957.

————. *Helping,* edited by Helen Harris Perlman. Chicago: University of Chicago Press, 1969.

Whitehorn, John C. "Guide to Interviewing and Clinical Personality Study." *Archives of Neurology and Psychiatry* 52 (September 1944): 197-216.

Wilson, Suanna J. *Confidentiality in Social Work: Issues and Principles.* New York: The Free Press, 1978.

————. *Recording.* New York: The Free Press, 1980.

Zentner, Ervin B. "The Use of Letters To Sustain the Casework Process." *Social Casework* 48 (March 1967): 135-40.